# START Listening

**WorldCom Edu**

Kim Jisun, Jason Cha

© 2009 published by WorldCom Edu.

All rights reserved. No part of this book may be
reproduced, stored in a retrieval system, or transmitted
in any form or by any means, electronic, mechanical,
photocopying, recording, or otherwise, without prior
permission in writing from the publisher.

ISBN : 978-89-6198-171-2

**Desk Copy Request / Information**
To place your desk copy request or for more information,
please contact the following office:
Tel : (02) 3273-4300    Fax : (02) 3273-4303
Homepage : www.wcbooks.co.kr

# Contents

# Shopping

SL3-01
MP3

## Building Vocabulary

**Fill in the blanks with the words in the box.**

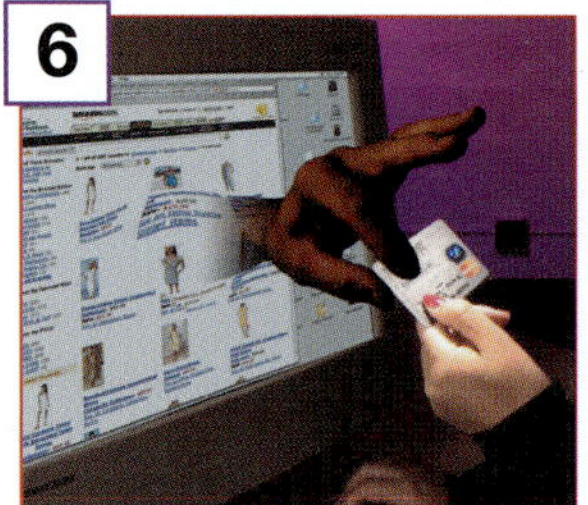

| | | | |
|---|---|---|---|
| wrap | receipt | discount | online shopping |
| cash | coupon | credit card | window shopping |

## Warming up

**Practice the dialogs using the expressions in the box.**

> ❶ buy a gift for my brother       ❷ I lost the receipt
>
> ❸ your Christmas shopping          ❹ I tried getting a refund for

**1**

**M**   Have you done all of ____________ yet?

**W**   Not yet.  I still have to ____________ .

**M**   You'd better buy it soon.  Christmas is next week.

**W**   That's okay because I know what to get him.

**2**

**M**   I can't believe the salesperson won't let me get a refund.

**W**   Why, what happened?

**M**   ____________ this jacket I bought.  But ____________ .

**01 / Unit1**
Listen and answer   **Listen and check your answers.**

**A** 02 / Unit1
Listen and answer  **Listen to the dialogs and number the correct pictures.**

**[1-4]**  **Which picture best describes the dialog?**

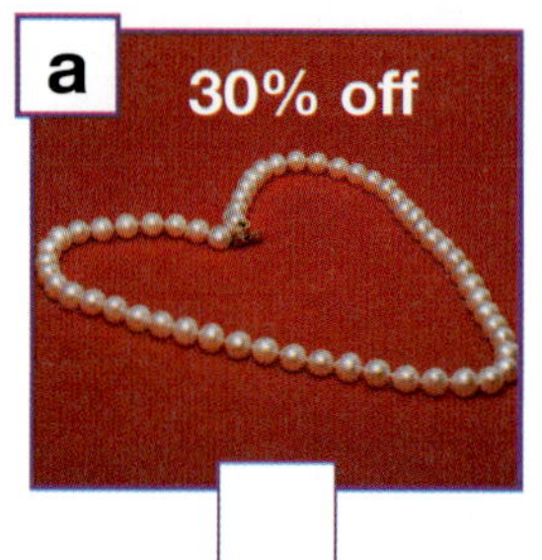

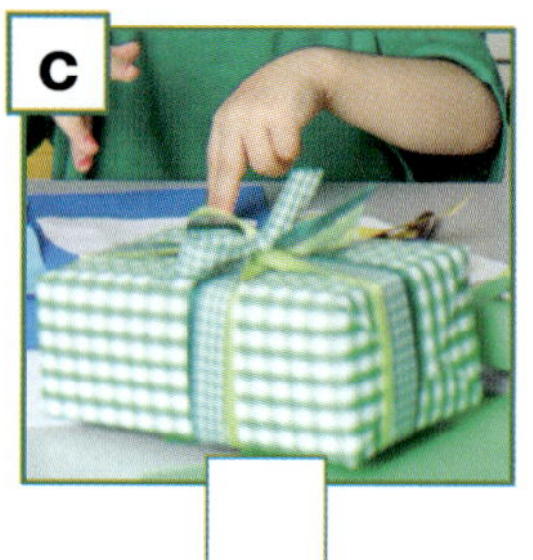


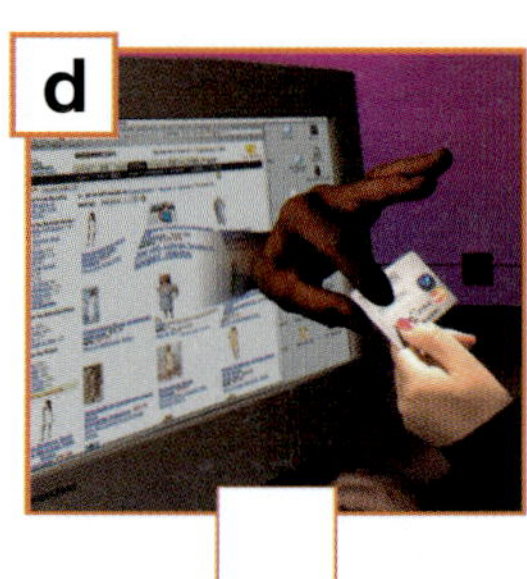


**B** 03 / Unit1
Listen and answer  **Listen to the dialogs and answer the questions.**

**[1-4]**  **Check the right statement.**

**1**  ☐  The man wears a size 10.

☐  The man wants to get a refund for his shirt.

**2**  ☐  The girl wants to get a new MP3 player for Christmas.

☐  The girl bought her MP3 player during a Christmas sale.

**3**  ☐  They're having a big sale on basketballs.

☐  They're having a buy two get one free sale on shoes.

**4**  ☐  The boy got his leather jacket from his uncle.

☐  The boy bought a used jacket at a garage sale.

# Conversation

**A**   **04** / Unit1
Listen and answer    **Listen to the dialog and answer the questions.**

**1**    Why did the woman come to the store?

    ⓐ To get a refund

    ⓑ To buy a t-shirt on sale

    ⓒ To exchange some clothes

**2**    What's the problem with the jeans?

    ⓐ They're the wrong size.

    ⓑ They're the wrong color.

    ⓒ They have a rip.

**B**   **05** / Unit1
Listen and answer    **Listen to the dialog and answer the questions.**

**1**    What does the man want?

    ⓐ A discount       ⓑ A coupon       ⓒ A free hat

**2**    Which of the following is NOT true?

    ⓐ The man received a 10% discount.

    ⓑ The man does not want the free hat.

    ⓒ The man is a member of the store.

# Passage

 **Listen to the passage and answer the questions.**

**1** What are Gina's favorite types of hats?

a

b

c

**2** How did Gina order the Italian soccer team hat?

ⓐ She went to Italy to but it.

ⓑ She bought it online.

ⓒ She asked her friend.

**3** Which of the following is NOT true?

ⓐ Gina has more than 200 hats.

ⓑ Gina buys hats in stores and online.

ⓒ Gina gives her hats to her best friends.

# Passage

   **Listen to the passage and answer the questions.**

**1  What is window shopping?**

ⓐ When you buy everything

ⓑ When you spend all your money

ⓒ When you look at things you want to buy

**2  Which of the following is true?**

ⓐ You can't always go window shopping.

ⓑ Window shopping is a popular hobby for many people.

ⓒ You need a lot of money to go window shopping.

**3  What is a shopping spree?**

ⓐ When you buy many things

ⓑ When you don't spend money

ⓒ When you try on clothes

#  Phone Calls

## Building Vocabulary

**Fill in the blanks with the words in the box.**

| 1 | 2 | 3 | 4 |
|---|---|---|---|
|  |  |  |  |

| 5 | 6 | 7 | 8 |
|---|---|---|---|
|  |  |  |  |

| send message | display | operator | cell phone |
|---|---|---|---|
| battery | text message | take a message | dial number |

## Practice the dialogs using the expressions in the box.

❶ on the other line

❷ I can take a message

❸ Give me a call back later

❹ I'll give him the message

**1**

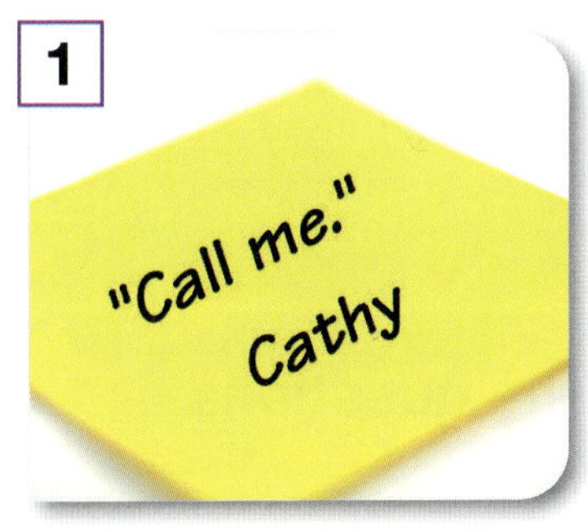



W   Hi, this is Cathy. Is Jordan there?

M   Hi Cathy. This is Jordan's dad. He's out right now but ______________.

W   OK, thanks. Please tell him to call me back.

M   ______________.

**2**

W   Hey Mark, it's me, Jane. I just got a new board game. It's really fun!

M   Sorry Jane, but I'm talking to Steve ______________.

W   That's okay. ______________.

M   OK. I'll call you later.



**Listen and check your answers.**

# Strategy



**A**  **09** / Unit2
Listen and answer   **Listen to the dialogs and number the statements.**

**[1-4]**   **Which best describes the situation?**

| | |
|---|---|
| _________ | The girl wants to know the number for the pizzeria. |
| _________ | The girl is going to send a text message to Steve. |
| _________ | The boy wants to know who called him from New York. |
| _________ | Ethan is doing his homework and can't talk to Jennifer. |

**B**  **10** / Unit2
Listen and answer   **Listen to the dialogs and answer the questions.**

**[1-4]**   **Check the right statement.**

**1**   ☐ The girl left a message for John.

☐ The girl took a message for John.

**2**   ☐ Mike is going bowling late in the afternoon.

☐ Mike is not going bowling because of an English test.

**3**   ☐ The woman has a problem with her Internet.

☐ The woman needs to wait another 20 minutes.

**4**   ☐ The man has the right number.

☐ Bobby Smith does not work at that office.

**A** **11** / Unit2
Listen and answer **Listen to the dialog and answer the questions.**

**1** **Which of the following is true?**

ⓐ Ms. Lane's line is busy.

ⓑ James is in a meeting right now.

ⓒ The man will not call her back.

**2** **What is the man's phone number?**

➡ _______________________________________________

**B** **12** / Unit2
Listen and answer **Listen to the dialog and answer the questions.**

**1** **Why is the boy's phone not working?**

ⓐ The display is broken.

ⓑ The battery ran out.

ⓒ It's out of the service area.

**2** **What is wrong with the girl's phone?**

ⓐ She dropped her phone.

ⓑ It's out of battery.

ⓒ She left it at home.

# Passage

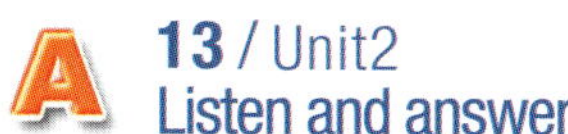

   **Listen to the passage and answer the questions.**

**1**   **Why did Linda call Mr. Baker?**

ⓐ To reschedule his doctor's appointment

ⓑ To cancel the appointment

ⓒ To tell him the schedule is full

**2**   **When is the earliest that Mr. Baker can see the Doctor?**

ⓐ Next week on Thursday

ⓑ Next week on Friday

ⓒ Next month

**3**   **What's wrong with Doctor Kim's office?**

ⓐ The doctor is too busy.

ⓑ The doctor is very sick.

ⓒ There are too many patients.

**B** **14** / Unit2
Listen and answer **Listen to the passage and answer the questions.**

**1** Which cell phone feature does the speaker talk about?

ⓐ Internet & Text message

ⓑ Watching TV

ⓒ Downloading music

**2** What does the speaker think about cell phones?

ⓐ They have made our lives better.

ⓑ Children should have their own.

ⓒ They are bad for our health.

**3** What does the speaker think of text messaging?

ⓐ It takes too much time.

ⓑ It is easy and fast.

ⓒ It is cheap but difficult .

# Personality

## Building Vocabulary

**Fill in the blanks with the words in the box.**

| | | | |
|---|---|---|---|
| **1**  | **2**  | **3**  | **4**  |
| **5**  | **6**  | **7**  | **8**  |

| | | | |
|---|---|---|---|
| shy | kind | excited | sociable |
| brave | annoyed | funny | disappointed |

## Practice the dialogs using the expressions in the box.

> ❶ I'm so depressed
> ❷ I was really annoyed
> ❸ look on the bright side
> ❹ I don't get angry easily

**1**

**M** It's April Fools' Day!

**W** Last year someone put glue on my chair. ______________ . Do you remember?

**M** Of course, I remember. I was the one who did it.

**W** That was you? You're lucky ______________ .

**2**

**W** ______________ . I hate it when it rains.

**M** The rain will stop soon and help the pretty flowers grow.

**W** I don't think it will stop raining anytime soon.

**M** We can't change the weather, so try to ______________ .

**15** / Unit3
Listen and answer

**Listen and check your answers.**

**A** 16 / Unit3
Listen and answer   **Listen to the speakers and number the correct pictures.**

**[1-4]   Who is the speaker describing?**

**B** 17 / Unit3
Listen and answer   **Listen to the dialogs and answer the questions.**

**[1-4]   Choose the right answer.**

**1   The boy is ____________.**

☐ careful        ☐ helpful        ☐ impatient

**2   The boy thinks Gina is ____________.**

☐ selfish        ☐ generous        ☐ smart

**3   The girl is ____________ because of her test results.**

☐ happy        ☐ excited        ☐ disappointed

**4   The man is ____________ to see his old friend.**

☐ excited        ☐ upset        ☐ relaxed

# Conversation

**A**  18 / Unit3  Listen and answer  **Listen to the dialog and answer the questions.**

**1**  Why was the boy late for class?

ⓐ He went to bed late.

ⓑ He thought it was Sunday.

ⓒ His mom didn't wake him up.

**2**  Why is the boy depressed?

ⓐ His favorite team lost the game.

ⓑ His teacher got angry at him.

ⓒ His mother punished him because he stayed up late.

**B**  19 / Unit3  Listen and answer  **Listen to the dialog and answer the questions.**

**1**  What does the boy think of Angie?

ⓐ She is smart, but selfish.

ⓑ She is brave, but lazy.

ⓒ She is sociable and brave.

**2**  Why does the boy think like above?

➡ Because ______________________________________

# Passage



**Listen to the passage and answer the questions.**

**1** Fill in the blanks with the right words.

> • The speaker is talking about the relation between
>
> ⓐ _________________ and our ⓑ _________________ .

**2** Draw a line to make a true statement.

ⓐ Green means •          • you have many friends.

ⓑ Black means •          • you are funny and smart.

ⓒ Purple means •          • you are very shy.

**3** If your friend likes red, what is he like?

ⓐ He is full of energy.

ⓑ He gets angry easily.

ⓒ He is very jealous.

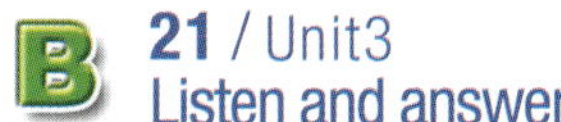

**B** 21 / Unit3
Listen and answer      **Listen to the passage and answer the questions.**

**1**    **Which of the following is true?**

    ⓐ Emily and Stella have similar personalities.

    ⓑ Emily and Stella are very different.

    ⓒ Susie prefers Emily over Stella.

**2**    **Write E if the statement refers to Emily, and S if it refers to Stella.**

    ⓐ ______________ is very funny.

    ⓑ ______________ is a quiet girl.

    ⓒ ______________ wants to be a famous writer.

    ⓓ ______________ wants to be a comedic actress.

**3**    **What is true about the three of them together?**

    ⓐ They argue a lot.

    ⓑ They have a lot of fun.

    ⓒ They can never agree.

# Healthy Life

SL3-04
MP3

## Building Vocabulary

**Fill in the blanks with the words in the box.**

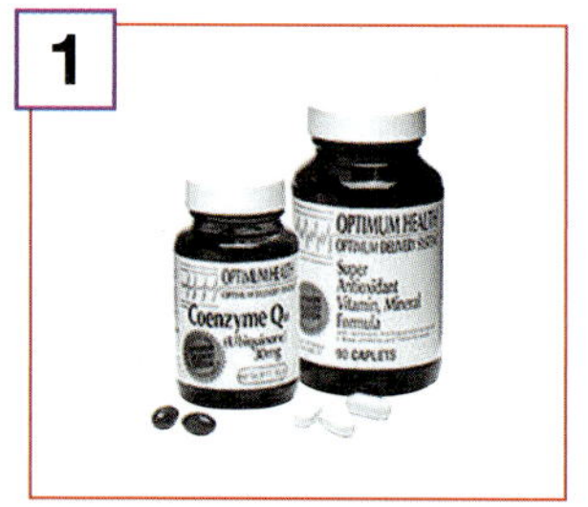

| fat | thin | exercise | dairy products |
| vegetarian | meats | vitamin | food pyramid |

## Practice the dialogs using the expressions in the box.

| | |
|---|---|
| ❶ went on a diet | ❷ tries to eat healthy foods |
| ❸ lives a very healthy life | ❹ wants to be thin like the models |

**1** 

**M**  Did you watch the news last night?  A woman turned 128 years old yesterday.

**W**  Wow, people are living much longer nowadays.

**M**  She ______________.  She exercises every day and ______________.

**2** 

**W**  Another one of my friends ______________.  Do you remember Kate?

**M**  I do, but she isn't fat.

**W**  She thinks that she is fat.  She always reads fashion magazines and ______________.

    **Listen and check your answers.**

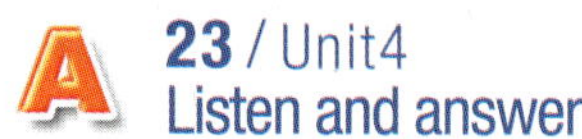

**A** 23 / Unit4
Listen and answer    **Listen to the dialogs and number the correct pictures.**

**[1-4]**   What is each person going to do to be healthy?

**B** 24 / Unit4
Listen and answer    **Listen to the dialogs and answer the questions.**

**[1-4]**   Check the right statement.

**1**   ☐   The steak in the sandwich tasted bad.

☐   His mom made the sandwich with tofu instead of meat.

**2**   ☐   The woman is going to rest at home.

☐   The woman is taking a yoga class with the man.

**3**   ☐   The man is going jogging every morning.

☐   The man stopped eating ice cream and snacks.

**4**   ☐   The woman enjoyed the steak made out of tofu.

☐   The woman can't eat the food because of the blood test.

# Conversation

**A** **25** / Unit4
Listen and answer    **Listen to the dialog and answer the questions.**

**1**  **Choose the food the woman probably doesn't eat.**

**2**  **Which of the following is true?**

ⓐ The man is a fruitarian.

ⓑ They both enjoy meats.

ⓒ The woman is a vegetarian.

**B** **26** / Unit4
Listen and answer    **Listen to the dialog and answer the questions.**

**1**  **What problem does the man have?**

ⓐ He lacks vitamins.

ⓑ He is very stressed because of work.

ⓒ He skips meals because he's very busy.

**2**  **What does the woman tell Jim to do?**

ⓐ Exercise regularly.

ⓑ Eat fruits, vegetables, and milk.

ⓒ Rest and get enough sleep.

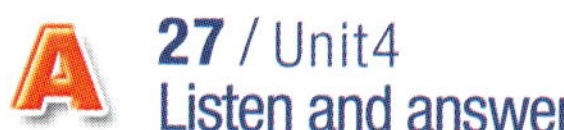

# Passage

 **Listen to the passage and answer the questions.**

**1** **What should be the biggest part of our diet?**

ⓐ Dairy

ⓑ Fats and sweets

ⓒ Bread and cereals

**2** **What should be the smallest part of our diet?**

ⓐ Meats

ⓑ Vegetables

ⓒ Fats and sweets

**3** **What is the food pyramid?**

ⓐ A type of vegetable

ⓑ A guide to eating healthy

ⓒ A type of healthy food

# Passage

 **Listen to the passage and answer the questions.**

**1** **Who can eat cheese?**

ⓐ Vegans

ⓑ Vegetarians

ⓒ Both of a and b.

**2** **Which of the following is true about vegans?**

ⓐ They enjoy food from an animal.

ⓑ They enjoy vegetables, but sometimes eat meat.

ⓒ They don't eat anything that comes from an animal.

**3** **Why are vegetarians and vegans so healthy?**

- They eat lots of ⓐ _______________________ and they

  never eat ⓑ _______________________ .

# Being Sick

## Building Vocabulary

**Fill in the blanks with the words in the box.**

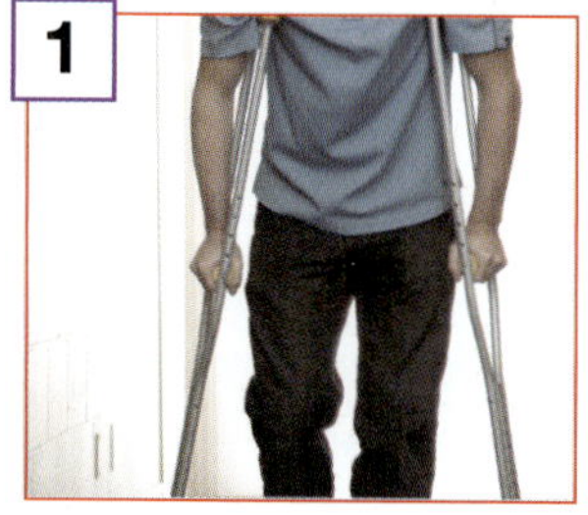
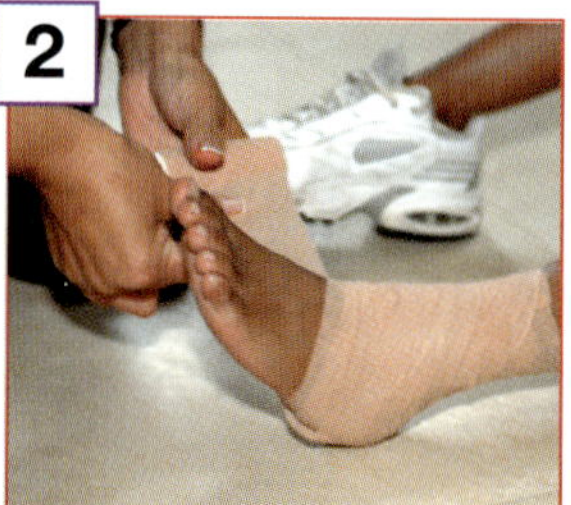
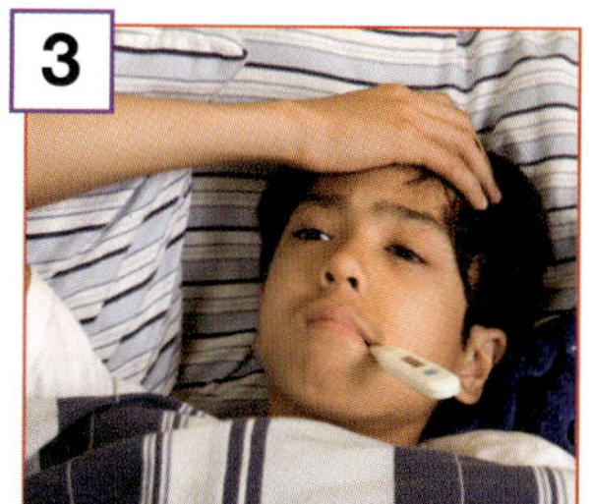
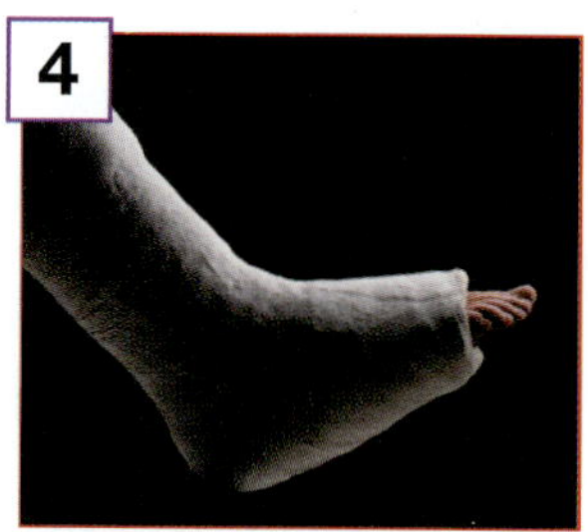

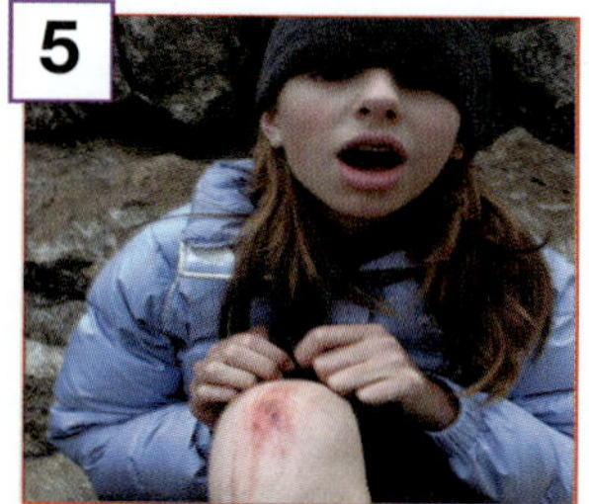

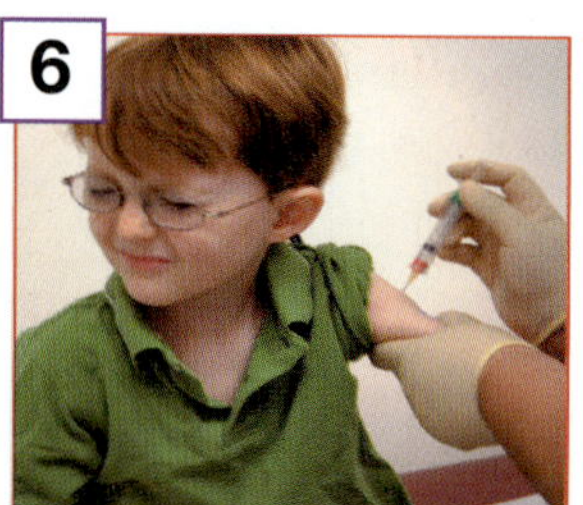

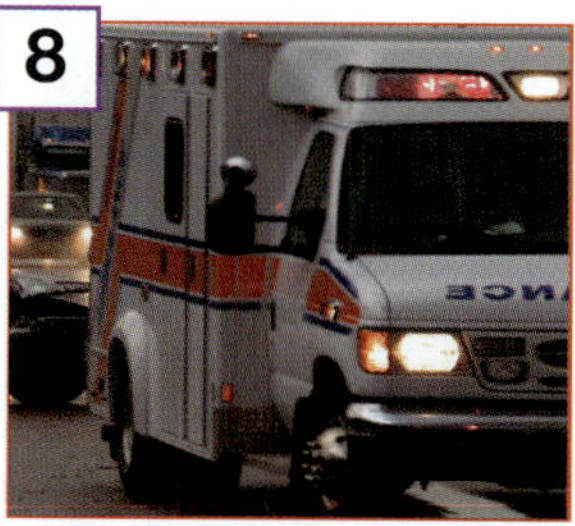

| | | | |
|---|---|---|---|
| cast | scrape | high fever | ambulance |
| sprain | crutches | injection | emergency room |

## Practice the dialogs using the expressions in the box.

❶ I hurt my leg
❷ It's just a bad sprain
❸ I have to use these crutches
❹ Everyone falls off a bike

**1** 

**M**   I can't believe this happened. I never fall.

**W**   _______________ . You'll be okay.

**M**   Yeah, I'm lucky I didn't break my arm. _______________ .

**W**   In a few weeks, you can ride a bike again.

**2** 

**W**   Oh no! Are you okay? What happened to you?

**M**   I'm okay. _______________ during the football game. Now _______________ for a month.

**W**   That's terrible.

**M**   No way. Once my leg heals, I can play football again.



**Listen and check your answers.**

**A** 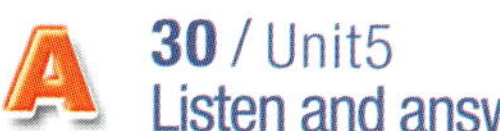
**30** / Unit5
Listen and answer — **Listen to the dialogs and number the correct pictures.**

**[1-4]**  **What's wrong with each person?**

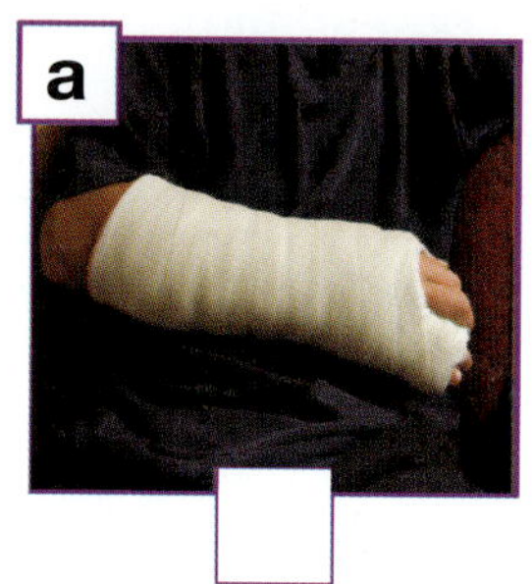

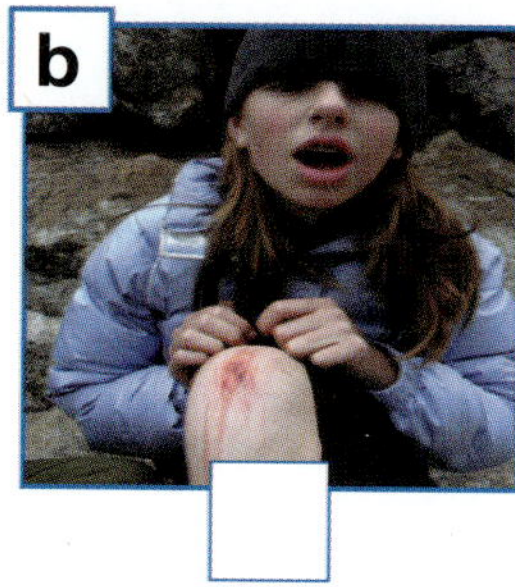

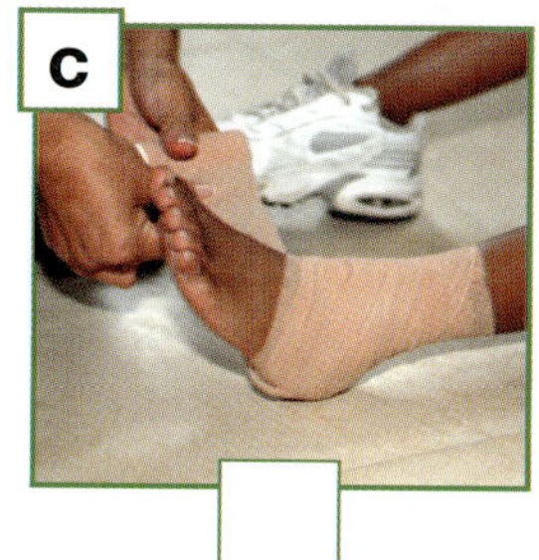

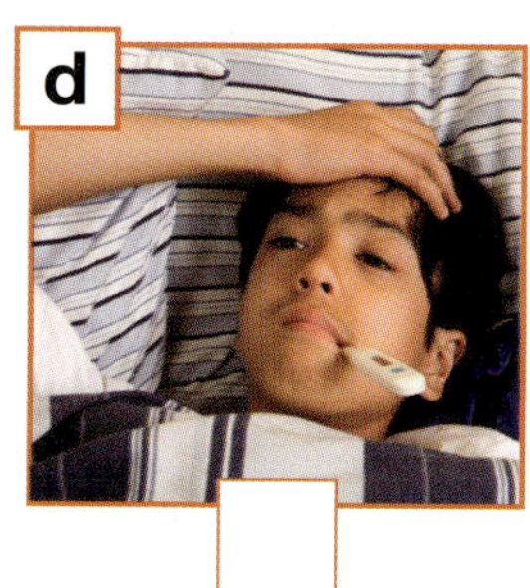

**B** 
**31** / Unit5
Listen and answer — **Listen to the dialogs and answer the questions.**

**[1-4]**  **Check the right statement.**

**1**  ☐ The boy had surgery done and it hurt a lot.

☐ The boy is going to have surgery tomorrow.

**2**  ☐ The player got hurt on his right thigh.

☐ The player fell down and he broke his right leg.

**3**  ☐ The boy went to the hospital because of a bad cold.

☐ The boy had a car accident and hurt his face and neck.

**4**  ☐ The doctor gave Jimmy a shot.

☐ The doctor put a bandage on the cut.

# Conversation

  **Listen to the dialog and answer the questions.**

**1** Who is probably the man?

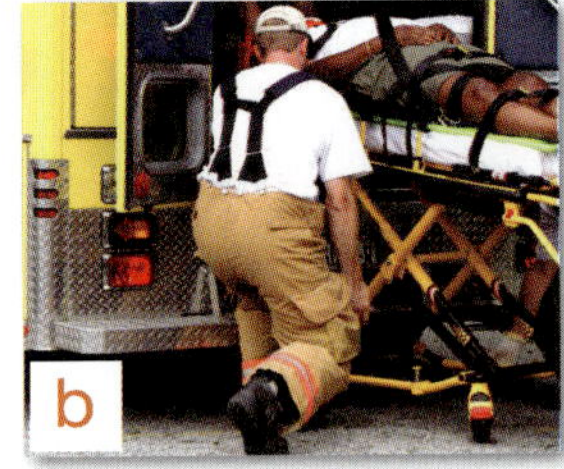


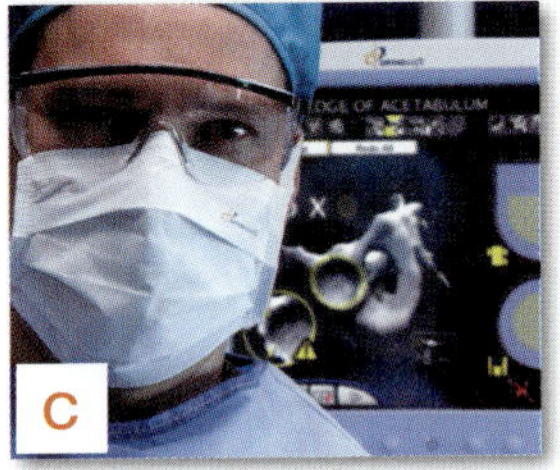


**2** Why did the man go to the hospital?

ⓐ He had a backache.

ⓑ His right wrist hurts.

ⓒ He is very stressed from work.

  **Listen to the dialog and answer the questions.**

**1** Choose a symptom the boy is NOT showing.

ⓐ Sneezing          ⓑ Fever          ⓒ Headache

**2** What can you tell from the dialog?

ⓐ The boy will get an injection.

ⓑ The boy will just stay at home.

ⓒ The boy will go to the hospital in an ambulance.

# Passage



**A** **34** / Unit5
Listen and answer　**Listen to the passage and answer the questions.**

**1**　What is the speaker mainly talking about?

ⓐ Various hospitals

ⓑ The busiest doctors

ⓒ The emergency room

**2**　Who are the busiest people at the hospital?

➡ ______________________________

**3**　When do you go to the emergency room?

ⓐ When you have a cold

ⓑ When you have a serious problem

ⓒ When the hospital is busy

# Passage



**Listen to the passage and answer the questions.**

**1** What is the speaker mainly talking about?

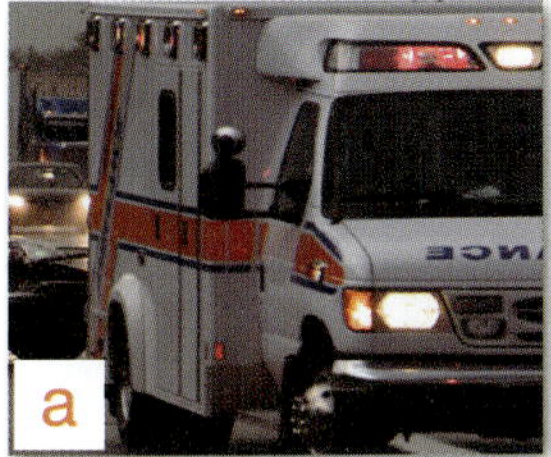  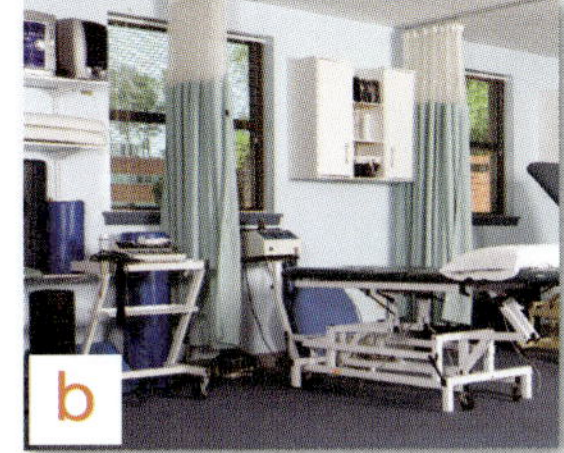  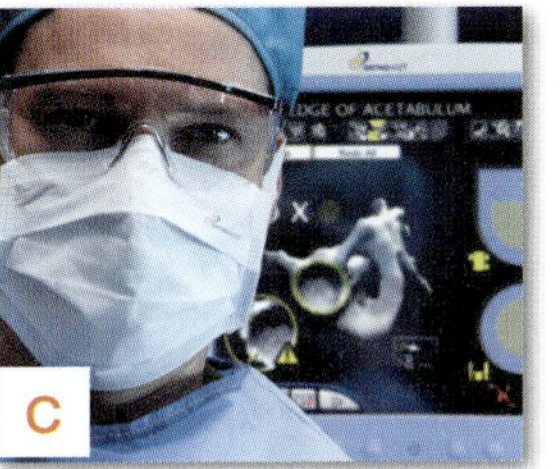

**2** What is an EMT?

  ⓐ An ER doctor

  ⓑ An ambulance doctor

  ⓒ An ambulance driver

**3** What do you need to know to be an EMT?

  ⓐ How to drive safe

  ⓑ How to help injured people

  ⓒ How to communicate with doctors

SL3-06
MP3

## Building Vocabulary

Fill in the blanks with the words in the box.

 1

2

 3

 4

 5

 6

 7

 8

| | | | |
|---|---|---|---|
| TV drama | drawing | video game | ride |
| cooking | puzzle | bungee jumping | model airplane |

## Practice the dialogs using the expressions in the box.

❶ That sounds like fun
❷ You really like that show
❸ my favorite TV drama
❹ What kind of game is it

**1** 

**M**  I got a new computer game today.  Do you want to try it?

**W**  Sure!  ______________?

**M**  It's a kind of car racing game.

**W**  ______________.

**2** 

**W₁**  Just ten more minutes until ______________!

**W₂**  ______________, don't you?

**W₁**  It's great.  The show has love, danger, jealousy......

**W₂**  All TV dramas are like that.



**Listen and check your answers.**

# Strategy



**37** / Unit6
Listen and answer

**Listen to the dialogs and number the correct pictures.**

**[1-4]**   What activity are they talking about?

   a

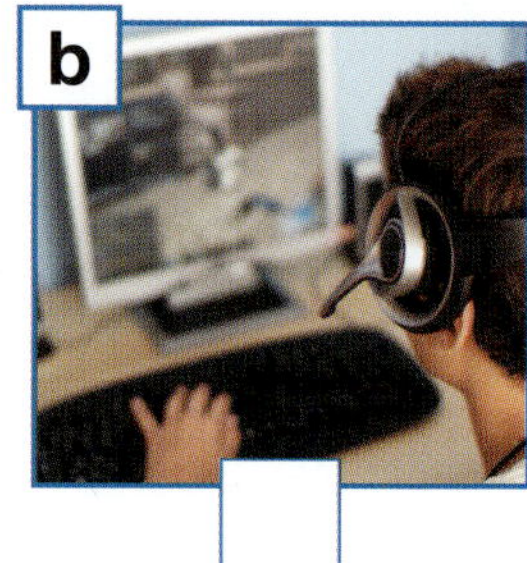   b

   c

   d



**38** / Unit6
Listen and answer

**Listen to the dialogs and answer the questions.**

**[1-4]**   Check the right statement.

**1**   ☐   The girl regrets joining the basketball team.

    ☐   The girl wants him to cheer as loud as he can.

**2**   ☐   The cooking class teacher doesn't cook very well.

    ☐   The woman enjoys her cooking class.

**3**   ☐   The boy could tell it was her dog in the picture.

    ☐   The boy's favorite toys are his red ball and Frisbee.

**4**   ☐   They both had a great time at the rock concert.

    ☐   The music was very loud at the rock concert.

# Conversation

**A**  **39** / Unit6
Listen and answer    **Listen to the dialog and answer the questions.**

**1**  **What does the man do every day?**

ⓐ Watch a movie        ⓑ Read comic books        ⓒ Play sports

**2**  **What do they agree on?**

ⓐ The movie is better than the comic book.

ⓑ Comic books are not fun.

ⓒ The book is better than the movie.

**B** **40** / Unit6
Listen and answer    **Listen to the dialog and answer the questions.**

**1**  **Why does the woman want to go to the arcade?**

ⓐ She loves video games.

ⓑ She loves stuffed animals.

ⓒ Her sister is there.

**2**  **Why do they need a lot of money?**

ⓐ The game is expensive.

ⓑ The game is hard.

ⓒ Taxis are expensive.

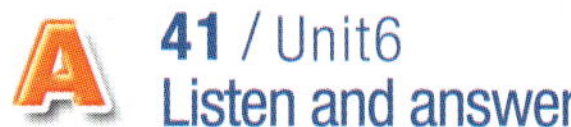



**A**  **Listen to the passage and answer the questions.**

**1**  **How many members does the Boy Scouts have?**

ⓐ 500

ⓑ 5,000

ⓒ 5 million

**2**  **Why do people think that Boy Scouts only learn outdoor skills?**

ⓐ Because they have class outside.

ⓑ Because they study animals and plants.

ⓒ Because they go camping and hiking.

**3**  **How do Boy Scouts learn life skills?**

ⓐ By studying nature

ⓑ By working together

ⓒ By doing exercise

# Passage

**B** **42** / Unit6
Listen and answer   **Listen to the passage and answer the questions.**

**1**   **When did bungee jumping first start?**

   ⓐ Early 1970's

   ⓑ Early 1980's

   ⓒ Early 1990's

**2**   **What's the most common mistake beginners make?**

   ⓐ They don't wear a helmet.

   ⓑ They choose a dangerous place.

   ⓒ The rope is too long.

**3**   **Which of the following is true?**

   ⓐ Beginners always use the right size rope.

   ⓑ Jumping off bridges is not allowed in most countries.

   ⓒ Bungee jumpers have jumped off the Eiffel Tower in Paris.

# Festivals

SL3-07
MP3



**Fill in the blanks with the words in the box.**

| | | | |
|---|---|---|---|
| marching band | book festival | music festival | street vendor |
| film festival | storytelling | pottery festival | masquerade |

## Practice the dialogs using the expressions in the box.

❶ see the marching band      ❷ selling balloons for the festival

❸ came out for the festival      ❹ this street so crowded before

**M**   Look at all these people that _____________ .

**W**   I've never seen _____________ .

**M**   How are we going to walk around?

**W**   I don't know but I'm hungry.  Let's try to walk towards the food.

**M**   Where did all these street vendors come from?

**W**   They came just for the festival.

**M**   That old man is _____________ .  Let's buy some.

**W**   Okay, but hurry. I want to _____________ .

**43** / Unit7
Listen and answer    **Listen and check your answers.**

**A** 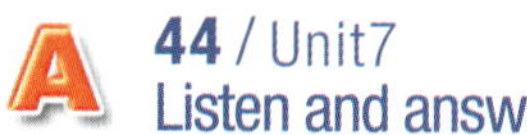
**44** / Unit7
Listen and answer

**Listen to the dialogs and number the correct pictures.**

**[1-4]** What kind of festival are they talking about?

**B** 
**45** / Unit7
Listen and answer

**Listen to the dialogs and answer the questions.**

**[1-4]** Check the right statement.

**1** ☐ The man can enter the area because he is in the parade.

☐ The man cannot enter the area because he lost his staff ID.

**2** ☐ The woman will go to the New York Photo Festival.

☐ The woman has an interview with a news reporter.

**3** ☐ They are going to the Jazz Festival together.

☐ The man is a volunteer at the Jazz Festival.

**4** ☐ The Storytelling Festival started in the early 1970s.

☐ The Storytelling Festival was started by a famous writer.

**A**  **46** / Unit7  
Listen and answer  **Listen to the dialog and answer the questions.**

**1**  **What's the man's job?**

    ⓐ Reporter for the Daily News

    ⓑ Film Festival staff

    ⓒ Security guard for the festival

**2**  **Why was the man not allowed to enter the room?**

    ⓐ He came too late.

    ⓑ He arrived too early.

    ⓒ He didn't have his ID card.

**B**  **47** / Unit7  
Listen and answer  **Listen to the dialog and answer the questions.**

**1**  **Why is the boy going to England?**

a

b

c

**2**  **Fill in the blanks with the right words.**

- The boy will attend ⓐ _________________ with ⓑ _________________ .

   **Listen to the passage and answer the questions.**

**1**   **What festival is the speaker mainly talking about?**

**2**   **Where is the festival held?**

➡ _______________________________________________

**3**   **Which of the following is NOT true?**

ⓐ People from all over the world come to Cannes.

ⓑ Famous actors never go to the Cannes Film Festival.

ⓒ The festival is a great opportunity for young filmmakers.

 **Listen to the passage and answer the questions.**

**1** How does John feel about the festival tomorrow?

    ⓐ He doesn't want to go.

    ⓑ He's very excited.

    ⓒ He's sad because he can't go.

**2** What is John's part in the parade?

**3** Why was John nervous at first?

    ⓐ People might stare at him.

    ⓑ He might make a mistake.

    ⓒ He might see his friends.

# Unit 8

# Home Appliances

SL3-08
MP3



**Fill in the blanks with the words in the box.**

| 1  | 2 | 3  | 4  |
| --- | --- | --- | --- |
| ___________ | ___________ | ___________ | ___________ |

| 5  | 6  | 7  | 8  |
| --- | --- | --- | --- |
| ___________ | ___________ | ___________ | ___________ |

| blender | radiator | vacuum cleaner | air conditioner |
| --- | --- | --- | --- |
| oven | microwave | refrigerator | remote control |

## Warming up

### Practice the dialogs using the expressions in the box.

> ❶ you have a dishwasher
> ❷ no one can come here to fix it
> ❸ Our air conditioner broke down
> ❹ I have to wash them by hand

**1** 

**M** You're so lucky ______________ in your house.

**W** Well, sometimes the dishes are still dirty so ______________.

**M** I always have to wash my dishes by hand. I want a dishwasher, too.

**2** 

**M** Why is it so hot in here?

**W** ______________. Since today is Sunday, ______________.

**M** Oh, my God. I don't want to be in a place with no air conditioner.

**50** / Unit8
Listen and answer

**Listen and check your answers.**

**A**  **51** / Unit8
Listen and answer  **Listen to the dialogs and number the correct pictures.**

**[1-4]**  **What appliance are they talking about?**

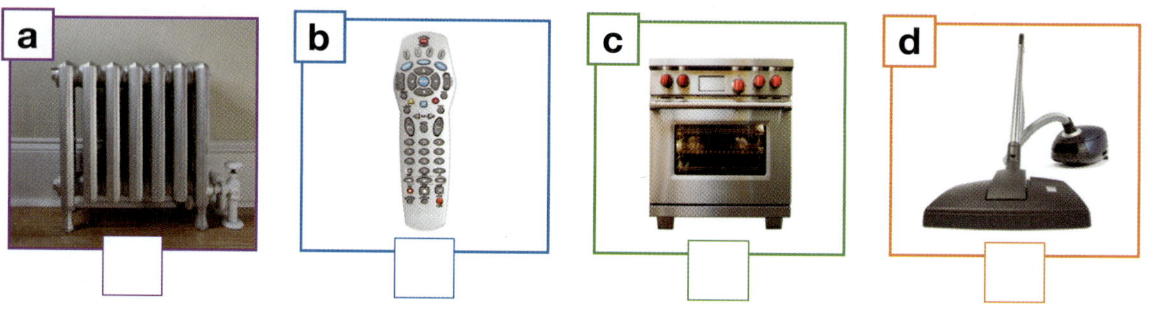


**B**  **52** / Unit8
Listen and answer  **Listen to the dialogs and answer the questions.**

**[1-4]**  **What is the problem? Choose the right answer.**

**1**  ☐ The boy's washer is broken.

☐ The boy went to the dry cleaner, but it was closed.

**2**  ☐ The blender is not working.

☐ There's no fruit in the refrigerator.

**3**  ☐ Their vacuum cleaner is broken.

☐ There's something wrong with their air conditioner.

**4**  ☐ The remote control is not for the new TV.

☐ The remote control ran out of batteries.

# Conversation

**A** 53 / Unit8
Listen and answer  **Listen to the dialog and answer the questions.**

**1** What's happening with the microwave?

ⓐ It stopped suddenly.

ⓑ It's making a loud sound.

ⓒ There are blue sparks in it.

**2** What caused this problem for the microwave?

ⓐ The man put a metal can in it.

ⓑ The man didn't close the door.

ⓒ The man heated the food for too long.

**B** 54 / Unit8
Listen and answer  **Listen to the dialog and answer the questions.**

**1** Why does the woman think the refrigerator is broken?

ⓐ The milk in the refrigerator is not cold.

ⓑ The meat in the refrigerator is rotten.

ⓒ The refrigerator makes a strange sound.

**2** Which of the following is true?

ⓐ The new refrigerator is not working well.

ⓑ The man spilled something on the motor.

ⓒ The man has had the refrigerator for a long time.

# Passage

 **Listen to the passage and answer the questions.**

**1   Why was the stove broken?**

ⓐ They used it too much.

ⓑ They spilled water on it.

ⓒ They didn't use it for a long time.


**2   Which of the following is NOT true?**

ⓐ They used the stove to heat up the water.

ⓑ Lisa will fix the broken stove by herself.

ⓒ Lisa's family likes to drink hot tea.


**3   How long couldn't they use the stove for?**

ⓐ Two days

ⓑ A week

ⓒ Two weeks

**B** 56 / Unit8
Listen and answer  **Listen to the passage and answer the questions.**

**1**   **What is the Roomba?**

   ⓐ A lawnmower

   ⓑ A vacuum cleaner

   ⓒ A dish washer

**2**   **Circle T for true and F for false.**

   ⓐ The Roomba moves all by itself.      **T**   **F**

   ⓑ The Roomba is small and quiet.      **T**   **F**

   ⓒ Sometimes the Roomba falls down stairs.      **T**   **F**

**3**   **What happens when a chair blocks the Roomba?**

   ⓐ The Roomba goes around it.

   ⓑ The Roomba starts beeping.

   ⓒ The Roomba shuts off.

# Environment

## Building Vocabulary

**Fill in the blanks with the words in the box.**

| 1 | 2 | 3 | 4 |
|---|---|---|---|
|  |  |  |  |

| 5 | 6 | 7 | 8 |
|---|---|---|---|
|  |  | 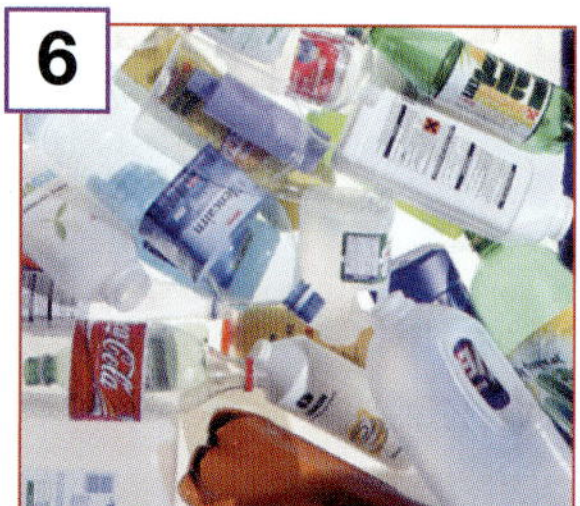 |  |

| | | | |
|---|---|---|---|
| recycling | metal can | trash bin | global warming |
| a bag of trash | water pollution | air pollution | empty bottles |

## Practice the dialogs using the expressions in the box.

> ❶ to the trash bin ❷ You forgot this bag of trash
>
> ❸ You have to recycle ❹ You can't put all of your trash

**1**

M Excuse me, madam.  You forgot something.

W I did?  What did I forget?

M ______________ . Please take it with you ______________ .

W I'm sorry.  I meant to bring it with me.

**2**

M ______________ in one bag.

W Why not?  It's all garbage.  What's wrong?

M ______________ . Put your plastics in a different bag.

W Okay.  Can you help me, please?

**57 / Unit9**
Listen and answer

## Listen and check your answers.

# Strategy



**58** / Unit9
Listen and answer   **Listen to the dialogs and number the correct pictures.**

**[1-4]**   **What are they talking about?**

**59** / Unit9
Listen and answer   **Listen to the dialogs and answer the questions.**

**[1-4]**   **Check the right statement.**

**1**   ☐  Sue always tries to save energy.

   ☐  Sue sometimes forgets to turn off the TV.

**2**   ☐  It's very cold outside since it's still February.

   ☐  It's February, but it's very warm outside.

**3**   ☐  They're upset because someone told them not to litter.

   ☐  They're upset because a man threw his garbage on the ground.

**4**   ☐  The man wants to move because of all the air pollution.

   ☐  The man thinks country life is much more fun.

# Conversation

 **60** / Unit9
Listen and answer **Listen to the dialog and answer the questions.**

**1**  Why are the polar bears dying?

    ⓐ Because people hunt them.

    ⓑ Because the water is polluted.

    ⓒ Because the Arctic ice is melting.

**2**  What are they worried about?

    ⓐ Global warming    ⓑ Water pollution    ⓒ Natural disasters

**B** **61** / Unit9
Listen and answer **Listen to the dialog and answer the questions.**

**1**  What are they talking about?

    ⓐ How to prevent air pollution

    ⓑ How to save our natural resources

    ⓒ How trash is dumped into the ocean

**2**  Why isn't plastic a natural resource?

    ⓐ Because it cannot be recycled.

    ⓑ Because it isn't separated.

    ⓒ Because it's made with chemicals.

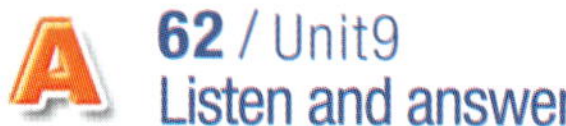

**A** **62** / Unit9
Listen and answer  **Listen to the passage and answer the questions.**

**1** **What is the speaker mainly talking about?**

   ⓐ Recycling

   ⓑ Pollution

   ⓒ Natural resources

**2** **Which of the following is NOT true?**

   ⓐ Glass is made from sand.

   ⓑ Food cannot be used again.

   ⓒ Metal cans can be recycled.

**3** **What is used to keep the soil healthy?**

   ⓐ Plants

   ⓑ Compost

   ⓒ Recycled cans and glasses

# Passage



**B** **63** / Unit9
Listen and answer

**Listen to the passage and answer the questions.**

**1   What destroys the ozone?**

a

b

c

**2   What does the ozone do?**

ⓐ Protects the Earth from the sun

ⓑ Saves people from air pollution

ⓒ Makes animals and plants healthy

**3   What is making the Earth hotter?**

ⓐ Compost

ⓑ Ozone

ⓒ Air pollution

# Famous People

SL3-10
MP3

## Building Vocabulary

**Fill in the blanks with the words in the box.**

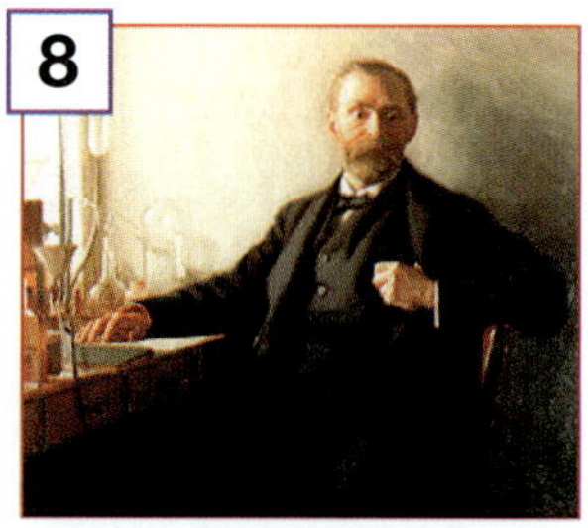

| President | athlete | inventor | film director |
| writer | musician | businessman | fashion designer |

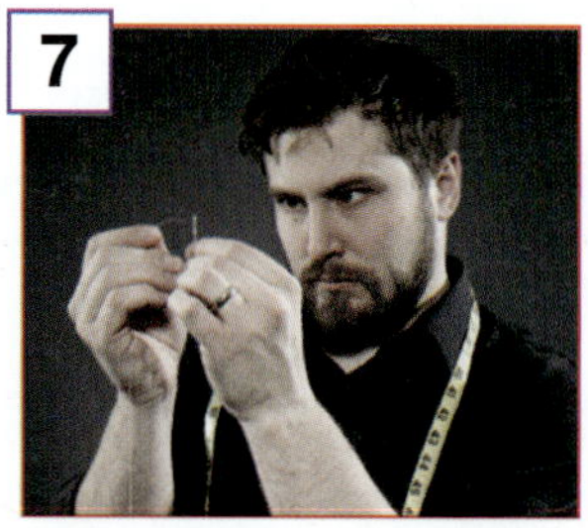

## Practice the dialogs using the expressions in the box.

> ❶ He's a great player     ❷ for the first time in history
>
> ❸ Hines Ward plays for them     ❹ we can tell our grandchildren one day

**1**

**W**   America might have a black president ____________ .

**M**   We voted for Barack Obama.  Isn't this exciting?

**W**   It sure is.  This is something ____________ .

**2**

**M**   Did you watch the football game yesterday? My favorite team won!

**W**   No, I didn't see it.

**M**   My favorite team is the Pittsburgh Steelers because ____________ .

**W**   Oh, I know who Hines Ward is. ____________ .

   **Listen and check your answers.**

# Strategy



**A**  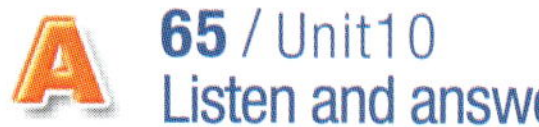 **Listen to the dialogs and number the correct pictures.**

**[1-4]**  Who are they talking about?

a 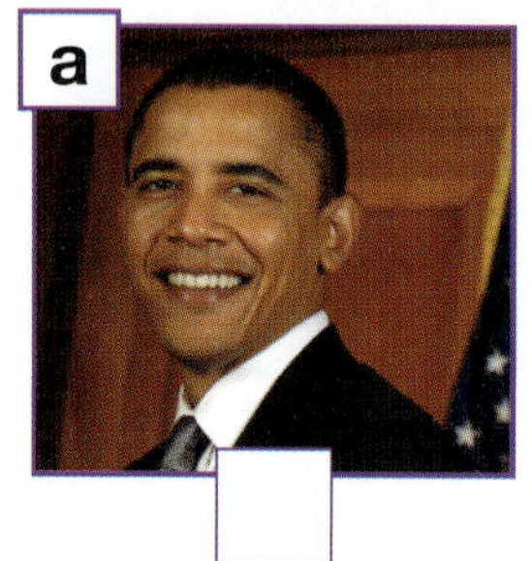  b   c 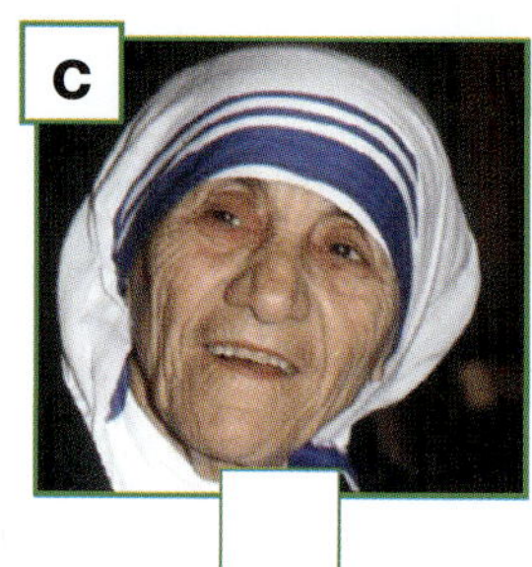  d 

**B**   **Listen to the dialogs and answer the questions.**



**[1-4]**  Check the right statement.

**1**  ☐ Park Tae Hwan won a gold medal in swimming at the Olympics.

☐ Park Tae Hwan was the first Korean to swim at the Olympics.

**2**  ☐ Steve Jobs made animated movies before working with computers.

☐ Steve Jobs used to own Pixar Animation Studios.

**3**  ☐ Prince Harry served in the Afghan war.

☐ Prince Harry got hurt when he was a soldier.

**4**  ☐ Mozart learned how to write piano songs when he was five.

☐ Mozart could play two instruments when he was five.

# Conversation

**A** **67** / Unit10
Listen and answer    **Listen to the dialog and answer the questions.**

**1**    How often are Nobel Prizes given?

ⓐ Every year          ⓑ Every three years          ⓒ Every five years

**2**    Which of the following is NOT true about Alfred Nobel?

ⓐ He was very poor.

ⓑ He invented dynamite.

ⓒ He started the Nobel Prize.

**B** **68** / Unit10
Listen and answer    **Listen to the dialog and answer the questions.**

**1**    What does the woman think of Walt Disney?

ⓐ He looks like Mickey Mouse.

ⓑ He is creative and funny.

ⓒ He has a deep voice.

**2**    Where did Mickey Mouse's personality come from?

ⓐ Walt Disney

ⓑ Walt Disney's friend

ⓒ A famous artist

# Passage

  **Listen to the passage and answer the questions.**

**1**  **What is the speaker mainly talking about?**

    ⓐ Bill Gates and his charity

    ⓑ Bill Gates and his family

    ⓒ Bill Gates and his company

**2**  **Which of the following is NOT true?**

    ⓐ The charity never gives away more than 1 billion dollars in a year.

    ⓑ The charity helps people in countries all over the world.

    ⓒ Bill Gates used millions of dollars on the charity.

**3**  **Who runs the charity with Bill Gates?**

    ➡ _______________________________________

 **Listen to the passage and answer the questions.**

**1 Who is Aesop?**

ⓐ He was a story writer for children.

ⓑ He was a Greek god.

ⓒ He is a character in a popular fable.

**2 What are the fables like?**

ⓐ They're long and difficult.

ⓑ They're short and scary.

ⓒ They teach a moral lesson.

**3 What is the moral of *The Ant and the Grasshopper*?**

ⓐ Work hard.

ⓑ Prepare for the future.

ⓒ Help others.

# Natural Disasters

SL3-11
MP3

## Building Vocabulary

**Fill in the blanks with the words in the box.**

| 1 | 2 | 3 | 4 |
|---|---|---|---|

_______________   _______________   _______________   _______________

| 5 | 6 | 7 | 8 |
|---|---|---|---|

_______________   _______________   _______________   _______________

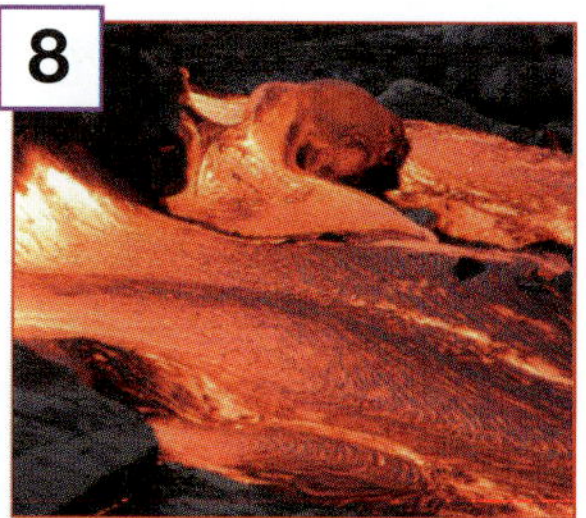

| flood | hail | volcano | drought |
| lava | wildfire | lightning | earthquake |

**Practice the dialogs using the expressions in the box.**

> ❶ We have to stay indoors
> ❷ There is a big storm coming
> ❸ There was an earthquake
> ❹ China should help those victims

**M** ______________ today.

**W** Why?  Is something wrong?

**M** ______________.  There will be lightning and thunder.

**W** Let's close all the windows and watch the news.

**W** ______________ in China this morning.

**M** Oh no!  Are the people there okay?

**W** Many people lost their homes.

**M** ______________ build new homes.

 **Listen and check your answers.**

**A** 72 / Unit11
Listen and answer   **Listen to the dialogs and number the correct pictures.**

**[1-4]**   **What natural disasters are they talking about?**

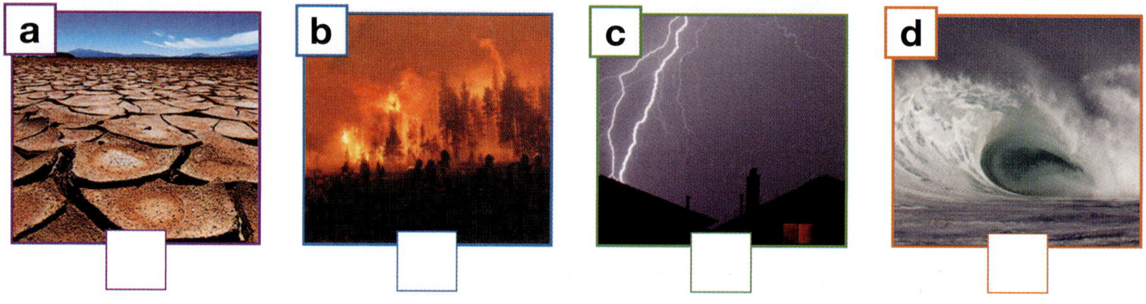



**B** 73 / Unit11
Listen and answer   **Listen to the dialogs and answer the questions.**

**[1-4]**   **Check the right statement.**

**1**   ☐ They should leave because there's a fire.

☐ They should stay under the table because of the earthquake.

**2**   ☐ The wind is very strong and the clouds are dark.

☐ The weatherman on the news said it is going to snow.

**3**   ☐ The weather forecaster said it's going to rain heavily.

☐ The weather forecaster said it's going to be cloudy, but won't rain.

**4**   ☐ The weatherman warned everyone about an earthquake.

☐ They'll stay home because of a severe thunderstorm.

# Conversation

**A** 74 / Unit11
Listen and answer    **Listen to the dialog and answer the questions.**

**1** **What is hail?**

 a

 b

 c

**2** **Why does the boy think that hail is dangerous?**

ⓐ It can cause a fire.

ⓑ It can break a window.

ⓒ It can ruin the crops.

**B** 75 / Unit11
Listen and answer    **Listen to the dialog and answer the questions.**

**1** **What are they talking about?**

ⓐ A fire in the forest

ⓑ A flood in town

ⓒ A snowstorm in the mountain

**2** **What made the disaster worse?**

ⓐ The wind          ⓑ The oil spill          ⓒ The man's mistake

# Passage



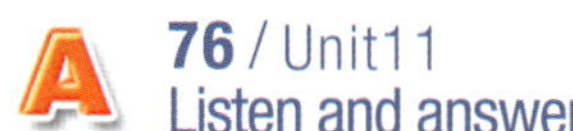

**A** Listen to the passage and answer the questions.

**1** Who helps disaster victims all over the world?

ⓐ FEMA

ⓑ United States

ⓒ The Red Cross

**2** How is the Red Cross different from FEMA?

ⓐ They help people all over the world.

ⓑ They raise money all over the world.

ⓒ They provide books and teachers to the young victims.

**3** What does FEMA give? Write three items.

➡ _______________________________

➡ _______________________________

➡ _______________________________

# Passage

**B** 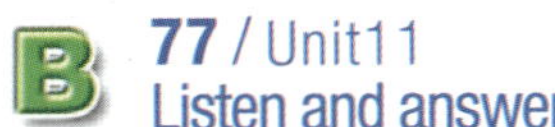 **77** / Unit11
Listen and answer    **Listen to the passage and answer the questions.**

**1**    **How is a volcano different from a mountain?**

   ⓐ There are no trees around it.

   ⓑ It is much bigger than a mountain.

   ⓒ It has a large opening at the top.

**2**    **According to the speaker, what is lava?**

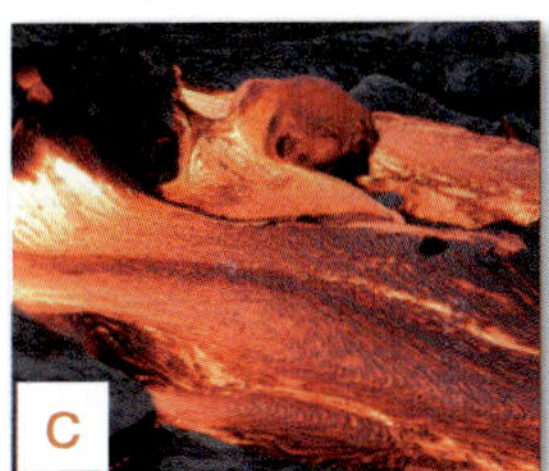


**3**    **Where does lava come from?**

   ⓐ From the ocean

   ⓑ From the fountain

   ⓒ From deep inside the earth

# Unit 12

# Outer Space

## Building Vocabulary

**Fill in the blanks with the words in the box.**

| 1 | 2 | 3 | 4 |
|---|---|---|---|
|  |  |  |  |
| _________ | _________ | _________ | _________ |

| 5 | 6 | 7 | 8 |
|---|---|---|---|
| 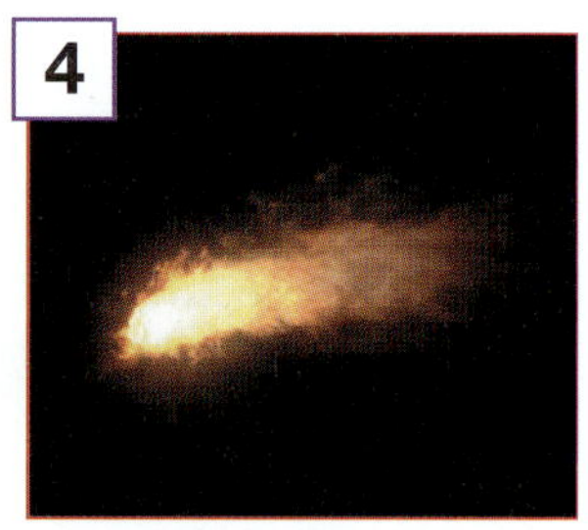 |  | 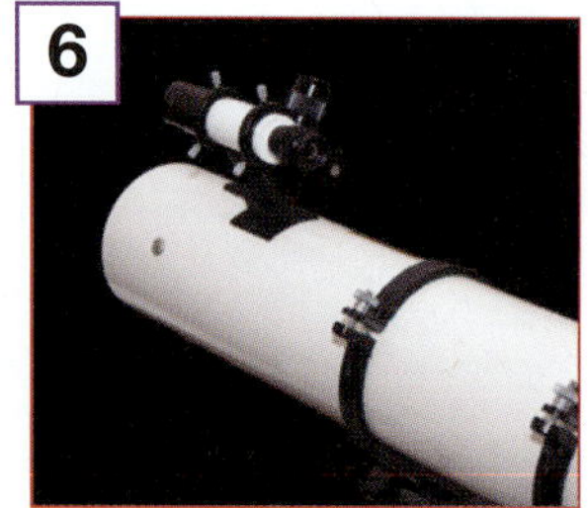 |  |
| _________ | _________ | _________ | _________ |

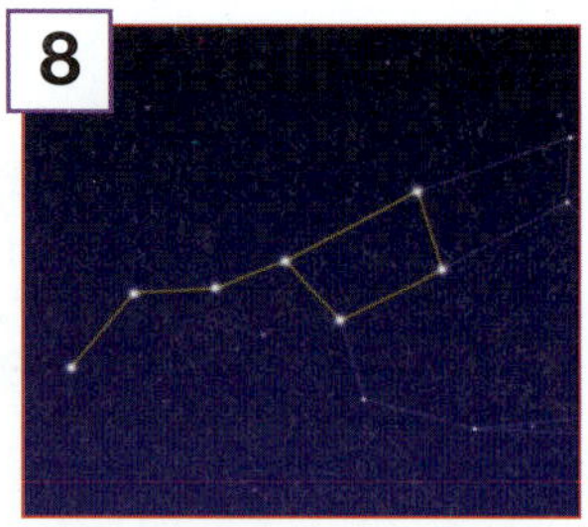

| | | | |
|---|---|---|---|
| Saturn | meteor | telescope | satellite |
| comet | Big Dipper | astronaut | space shuttle |

**Warming up**

**Practice the dialogs using the expressions in the box.**

> ❶ Did you see that meteor  ❷ aliens on other planets
>
> ❸ I want to be an astronaut  ❹ something living on another planet

**1**

M  ______________ last night?

W  Yeah, I did.  I even took a picture of it too.

M  I want to go to outer space some day.
   ______________ .

W  Maybe you will travel to Mars.

**2**

W  Do you think there might be ______________ ?

M  Sure, there could be ______________ .

W  In movies, aliens are always gray people with big eyes.  They look very funny.

M  Well, I'm sure to an alien we would look very funny too.



**Listen and check your answers.**

# Strategy

**A** **79** / Unit 12
Listen and answer    **Listen to the dialogs and number the correct pictures.**

**[1-4]**   **What are they talking about?**

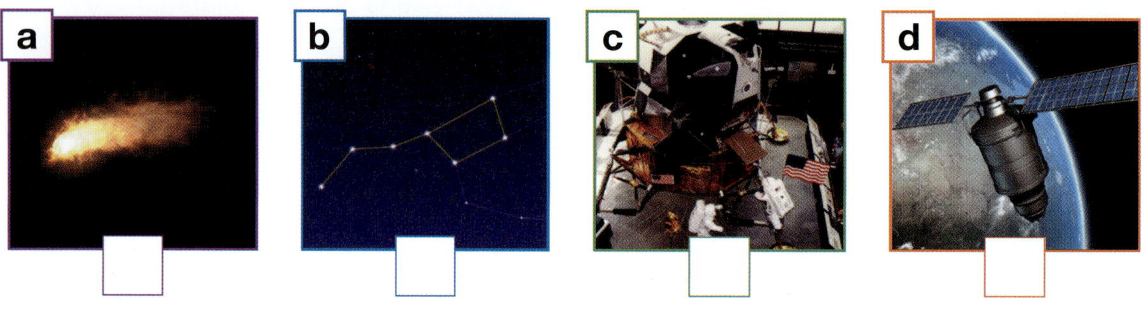



**B** **80** / Unit 12
Listen and answer    **Listen to the dialogs and answer the questions.**

**[1-4]**   **Check the right statement.**

**1**   ☐   The boy doesn't want to be an astronaut.

☐   The boy saw a comet when he was a kid.

**2**   ☐   The boy wants to see the whole solar system.

☐   The boy is happy just seeing the stars with his telescope.

**3**   ☐   Halley's Comet will come back in 2061.

☐   You can see Halley's Comet only with a telescope.

**4**   ☐   An astronaut goes into space.

☐   An astronomer builds spaceships.

**A** **81** / Unit12
Listen and answer    **Listen to the dialog and answer the questions.**

**1** **Which planet is Saturn?**

a

b

c

**2** **Why does the girl like Mars?**

ⓐ Because she likes SF movies.

ⓑ Because she likes its shape.

ⓒ Because she wants to go there someday.

**B** **82** / Unit12
Listen and answer    **Listen to the dialog and answer the questions.**

**1** **Why can't we see many meteors?**

ⓐ They are too small to see.

ⓑ They are too fast to see.

ⓒ They burn up before we can see them.

**2** **According to the speakers, what are meteors?**

a

b

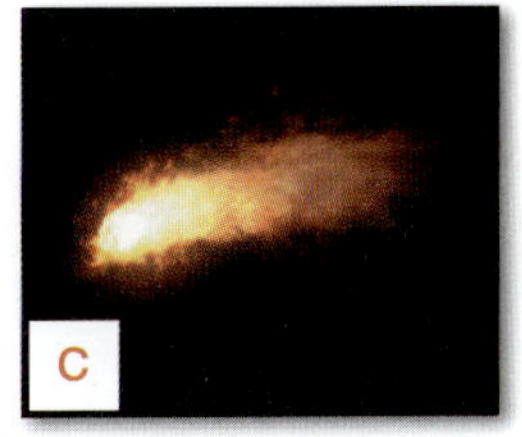
c

# Passage

   **Listen to the passage and answer the questions.**

**1**   **What do you call something that orbits the sun?**

   ⓐ Comet

   ⓑ Moon

   ⓒ Satellite

**2**   **Which of the following is true?**

   ⓐ Halley's Comet is the newest comet.

   ⓑ A comet is made of ice, dust, and rock.

   ⓒ Comets have bright wings.

**3**   **Why is Halley's Comet famous?**

   ⓐ Because it's the biggest comet.

   ⓑ Because it's the brightest comet.

   ⓒ Because you can see it with the naked eye.

# Passage

   **Listen to the passage and answer the questions.**

**1** Who is Neil Armstrong?

ⓐ An astronaut

ⓑ A person who studies stars

ⓒ A person who makes spaceships

**2** Which of the following is true about Neil Armstrong?

ⓐ He died in 1969.

ⓑ He went to the moon alone.

ⓒ He was the first man on the moon.

**3** What did Neil Armstrong do before he flew the space shuttle?

➡ ________________________________________

For Kids

START
Listening
Workbook
3
SL3-COVER
MP3
WorldCom Edu

# START Listening

## Workbook

3

WorldCom Edu

# Shopping



**A**   **Fill in the blanks with the right words in the box.**

1   ___________   completely new

2   ___________   to come to a certain place

3   ___________   to go to a different country

4   ___________   to change things with another person

5   ___________   to buy something and have it mailed to you

6   ___________   a reduction in the regular price of products

7   ___________   a person whose job is to sell things

8   ___________   a plastic card you use to buy goods on credit

9   ___________   when you return an item and get your money back

10   ___________   to cover completely with something, such as cloth or paper

11   ___________   manufactured animal skin used for clothes, bags, and furniture

12   ___________   a piece of paper you get in a shop as proof you bought something

| | | | |
|---|---|---|---|
| ❶ salesperson | ❷ receipt | ❸ refund | ❹ credit card |
| ❺ leather | ❻ brand-new | ❼ abroad | ❽ exchange |
| ❾ discount | ❿ arrive | ⓫ order | ⓬ wrap |

**1**   He's planning to study ______________ in France.

    ⓐ aboard     ⓑ absent     ⓒ abroad

**2**   Can I ______________ this book for a magazine?

    ⓐ change     ⓑ exchange     ⓒ charge

**3**   We are now selling all the books at a 20% ______________.

    ⓐ sell     ⓑ payment     ⓒ discount

**4**   If you ______________ earlier than me, go inside the building since it's cold.

    ⓐ receive     ⓑ arrive     ⓒ survive

**5**   I couldn't find the book at the store so I ______________ it online.

    ⓐ ordered     ⓑ paid     ⓒ cashed

**6**   Please ______________ the doll. It's a present for my sister.

    ⓐ clothe     ⓑ paper     ⓒ wrap

**7**   If you want to get a refund, you should bring your ______________.

    ⓐ receipt     ⓑ coupon     ⓒ gift card

**8**   If you find any fault, you can return it and receive a ______________.

    ⓐ refund     ⓑ exchange     ⓒ bill

**9**   You can pay for it with cash or ______________.

    ⓐ receipts     ⓑ coupons     ⓒ credit cards

**10**   I am saving money to buy high-quality ______________ boots.

    ⓐ leather     ⓑ wool     ⓒ cashmere

## Listen to the dialogs and fill in the blanks.

**A  04 / Unit1**
Listen and answer

W    Excuse me, I ___________ these blue jeans yesterday but they are

___________ ___________ .

M    Do you have your ___________ ?

W    Sure.  Here you are.

M    Would you like to ___________ ___________ ?

W    Yes, I want to exchange them for ___________ ___________ ___________ .

M    Sorry, those blue jeans are ___________ ___________ ___________ .

W    Oh, then I would like a ___________ .

M    Alright, just a minute.


**B  05 / Unit1**
Listen and answer

W    How does that ___________ , sir?

M    It feels great.  ___________ ___________ is perfect.  How much are these?

W    They are ___________ dollars, sir.

M    Wow.  That's expensive.  Can I ___________ ___________ ___________ ?

I'm a ___________ of this store.

W    No, we can't do that because they're not that expensive.  But I can give you

___________ ___________ ___________ if you buy them.

M    ___________ ___________ the shoes but you can ___________ the hat.

## Listen to the passages and fill in the blanks.

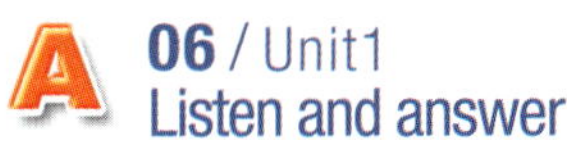

**A** **06** / Unit1
Listen and answer

Gina loves ____________ . She especially loves baseball caps.  She's ____________
over 200 hats.  ____________ ____________ ____________ are baseball caps.  She
bought them in ____________ and ____________ .  Sometimes she asks her friends
who ____________ ____________ to buy her a hat.  Gina has ____________
____________ ____________ hats.  A few days ago, she got a famous Italian soccer
team hat.  She wanted to ____________ ____________ for a long time.  When she
____________ found it on a ____________ ____________ , she ____________
____________ right away.  When the cap ____________ , Gina was so happy.

**B** **07** / Unit1
Listen and answer

Nowadays, shopping is a ____________ ____________ for many people.  On
weekends when you have nothing to do, you can ____________ ____________ .  And
don't worry if you don't have ____________ ____________ .  That's not a problem.
You can always go ____________ ____________ .  Window shopping is when you
____________ ____________ any money and only ____________ ____________ items.
You must be careful though.  Window shopping could ____________ ____________
a shopping spree.  At first, you may just look at things you want to buy.  But
____________ in the day you might actually ____________ ____________ of them!

# Phone Calls

SL3-02
MP3

## A. Fill in the blanks with the right words in the box.

1. __________ a sign sent to a person to give a message

2. __________ a telephone connection

3. __________ to know who a person is or what the thing is

4. __________ opposite of spend; to keep, usually for future use

5. __________ to plan again for another or later time

6. __________ communication sent by speech or writing

7. __________ to press the numbers on a telephone

8. __________ a small device that can provide power for electrical products

9. __________ to keep a telephone line open, to wait during a call

10. __________ a person who connects calls in places like a hotel or an office

11. __________ a series of numbers you need when you call a person in a different area

12. __________ additional numbers you dial to reach a specific person, usually at a company or an office

| ❶ line | ❷ area code | ❸ recognize | ❹ signal |
|---|---|---|---|
| ❺ message | ❻ operator | ❼ dial | ❽ battery |
| ❾ extension | ❿ reschedule | ⓫ save | ⓬ hang on |

**1**  The meeting will be ________________ from Monday to Wednesday.

ⓐ scheduled          ⓑ appointed          ⓒ rescheduled

**2**  If you want to be rich, you have to ________________ your money.

ⓐ bank          ⓑ save          ⓒ spend

**3**  I'm trying to reach the manager. Can you tell me her ________________?

ⓐ exit          ⓑ expert          ⓒ extension

**4**  When I was lost in the ocean, I sent a distress ________________.

ⓐ area          ⓑ signal          ⓒ symbol

**5**  I couldn't ________________ her at first sight.

ⓐ remind          ⓑ recognize          ⓒ require

**6**  It's urgent. ________________ 911 quickly.

ⓐ Sign          ⓑ Dial          ⓒ Signal

**7**  Can you give him a ________________ for me?  Tell him I'm going to be late.

ⓐ message          ⓑ notice          ⓒ sign

**8**  His ________________ is busy.  Would you like to leave a message?

ⓐ call          ⓑ phone          ⓒ line

**9**  Can I borrow your cell phone? My ________________ just died.

ⓐ battery          ⓑ signal          ⓒ area code

**10**  Please dial 9, and then the ________________ will help you.

ⓐ operator          ⓑ clerk          ⓒ salesperson

## Listen to the dialogs and fill in the blanks.

**A**  **11** / Unit2
Listen and answer

M   Hi, this is James.  Can I ____________ ____________ Ms. Lane?

W   ____________ ____________ is busy right now.  Do you want to ____________

____________ ____________ ?

M   No, I'll ____________ her ____________ a little later.  Wait, I ____________ that

I have a ____________ in 10 minutes. Could you please tell her I'll

____________ ____________ at 4:00?

W   Sure.  May I have your ____________ ____________ too, just in case?

M   My number is ____________ - ____________ .  And my ____________ is 201.


**B**  **12** / Unit2
Listen and answer

W   Hey, can I use your ____________ ?  I need to call my dad but my

____________ just ____________ ____________ .

M   My phone ____________ ____________ .  I don't know what's wrong.  I think

____________ ____________ .

W   Really?  Let me see.  Oh, it's not broken.  It says out of ____________

____________ .  There's ____________ ____________ here.

M   Well, that's good.  I thought I ____________ ____________ ____________ have

to buy a new phone.

## Listen to the passages and fill in the blanks.

**A**  **13** / Unit2
Listen and answer

Hello, this ___________ is ___________ Mr. Baker.  This is Linda ___________

Doctor Kim's office.  We're very sorry but we have to ___________ your

appointment.  Doctor Kim is very sick and ___________ ___________ be back

until next week.  The earliest we could reschedule your ___________ for is next

week on Thursday.  Please ___________ ___________ as soon as you can.  We

have many patients ___________ to reschedule.  If you wait ___________

___________ , our schedule might ___________ ___________ .  Our ___________

___________ are from 8 a.m. to 5 p.m.  Thank you very much.  Have a great day.


**B**  **14** / Unit2
Listen and answer

Nowadays ___________ ___________ have many more features than before.  If

you do not have time to talk for very long, you can ___________ a text message.

___________ ___________ is easy and it ___________ ___________ .  All you

have to do is ___________ your message and ___________ ___________ .  The

message will be ___________ almost instantly!  Some cell phones also let you

use the ___________ .  You can send ___________ and ___________ web sites.

You don't need to ___________ around your ___________ with you anymore.

Cell phones really ___________ ___________ our lives for the better.

# Unit 3

# Personality



**Vocabulary**

**A** **Fill in the blanks with the right words in the box.**

1 ___________ favored, fortunate

2 ___________ feeling angry or upset

3 ___________ sad, unhappy, unpleasant

4 ___________ feeling worried, stressed and uneasy

5 ___________ something that's hopeful or favorable

6 ___________ willing to do something without fear

7 ___________ uncomfortable or nervous with other people

8 ___________ clever; intelligent ; to be aware of many things

9 ___________ to be friendly with people; to have many friends

10 ___________ awkward when moving around; without skill and grace

11 ___________ feeling sad because something you wanted has not happened

12 ___________ to think of again;  keep in mind; remain aware of

| | | | |
|---|---|---|---|
| ❶ annoyed | ❷ lucky | ❸ bright side | ❹ nervous |
| ❺ remember | ❻ brave | ❼ wise | ❽ sociable |
| ❾ clumsy | ❿ disappointed | ⓫ depressed | ⓬ shy |

**B**   **Choose the right words for the blanks.**

**1**   If you want to be ______________ , you'd better read many books.

   ⓐ cheerful       ⓑ wise       ⓒ favorite

**2**   He failed the exam, so he was very ______________ with himself.

   ⓐ disappointed       ⓑ happy       ⓒ pleasant

**3**   What's wrong? You look so ______________ .

   ⓐ kind       ⓑ depressed       ⓒ sociable

**4**   The girl was too ______________ to speak to him.

   ⓐ lucky       ⓑ smart       ⓒ shy

**5**   They were ______________ about their interview.

   ⓐ nervous       ⓑ humorous       ⓒ generous

**6**   Do you have her number? I can't ______________ it.

   ⓐ notice       ⓑ remember       ⓒ recognize

**7**   He was so ______________ that he could save a boy from drowning.

   ⓐ selfish       ⓑ bright       ⓒ brave

**8**   He was ______________ to escape from the fire.

   ⓐ clumsy       ⓑ lucky       ⓒ shy

**9**   Emma is so ______________ that everyone at her school knows who she is.

   ⓐ sociable       ⓑ depressed       ⓒ childish

**10**   Meg is very ______________ . She spilled her milk and fell down the stairs today.

   ⓐ coward       ⓑ intelligent       ⓒ clumsy

## Listen to the dialogs and fill in the blanks.

**A** **18** / Unit3
Listen and answer

W   Hey, Jacob. ___________ ___________ again.  What time did you

___________ ___________ ___________ last night?

M   I went to bed at ___________ 3:00 a.m. I ___________ a soccer game

between Manchester United and Blackburn last night.

W   That's why you look so ___________.

M   I'm ___________ ___________. I'm ___________ because my teacher

___________ ___________ ___________ me this morning.

**B** **19** / Unit3
Listen and answer

M   How was your ___________ ___________ Venice, Angie?

W   It was great.  I've never seen such a ___________ ___________.

M   Did you travel ___________ ___________?

W   Yes, I did.  I like traveling ___________ because I have ___________

___________ to ___________ new people.

M   Wow, I've never been ___________ by myself.  You're a very ___________

and ___________ ___________, Angie.

W   I'm brave, but ___________ ___________ sociable.

**Listen to the passages and fill in the blanks.**

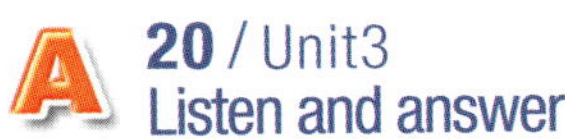

**20** / Unit3
Listen and answer

Everyone has a _____________ _____________ . Some people _____________ that favorite colors can tell you about _____________ . For example, if your favorite color is green, you might be sociable and have _____________ _____________ . If you like yellow, you could be _____________ and _____________ . If you like red, you could be _____________ and _____________ _____________ _____________ . And if you like black, you're probably _____________ and like to be by yourself. If you like _____________ , you might be _____________ and _____________ . So, what's your favorite color? Do you think that colors have something _____________ _____________ _____________ our personality?

**21** / Unit3
Listen and answer

Susie has two _____________ _____________ . They are Emily and Stella. Emily and Stella are very _____________ . Emily is a _____________ _____________ who likes reading books. Emily wants to be a famous _____________ such as J.K. Rowling. She _____________ _____________ her friends about the books _____________ _____________ . Stella is a funny girl who has a great _____________ _____________ _____________ . She always makes others _____________ when she tells a story. She wants to be a comedic _____________ . Emily and Stella may be very different, but the three of them always have a lot of _____________ _____________ .

# Unit 4 — Healthy Life



**Vocabulary**

**A** **Fill in the blanks with the right words in the box.**

1 ___________ not thick, slender

2 ___________ a place where you can exercise

3 ___________ overweight, plump, large

4 ___________ good for your health

5 ___________ people who never eat meat or fish

6 ___________ goods; merchandise; produce

7 ___________ to lose weight by eating healthy foods

8 ___________ something you take for more nutrition

9 ___________ to move your body to be healthy and strong

10 ___________ at a high level, at a difficult level where much skill is needed

11 ___________ someone who doesn't eat animals nor food that comes from an animal

12 ___________ a kind of exercise in which you pose in several positions and stay in those positions for a while

| | | | |
|---|---|---|---|
| ❶ diet | ❷ vitamins | ❸ advanced | ❹ vegan |
| ❺ vegetarian | ❻ product | ❼ yoga | ❽ exercise |
| ❾ thin | ❿ gym | ⓫ fat | ⓬ healthy |

## B Choose the right words for the blanks.

**1** It is important to ______________ every day for at least 30 minutes.

   ⓐ health        ⓑ drill        ⓒ exercise

**2** Gina is ______________ because all she eats are fruits and vegetables.

   ⓐ thin        ⓑ fat        ⓒ chubby

**3** Annie exercises at the ______________ every day.

   ⓐ gym        ⓑ clinic        ⓒ pool

**4** She's not ______________ nor chubby. She is a normal girl.

   ⓐ thin        ⓑ fat        ⓒ slim

**5** My grandparents try to eat ______________ foods such as milk, nuts, etc.

   ⓐ dairy        ⓑ healthy        ⓒ junk

**6** I don't like to eat vegetables so I take ______________ instead.

   ⓐ vitamins        ⓑ meals        ⓒ medicine

**7** The students in the ______________ music class can play songs by Mozart.

   ⓐ advanced        ⓑ modern        ⓒ developing

**8** He only eats vegetables and dairy products because he is a(n) ______________.

   ⓐ vet        ⓑ athlete        ⓒ vegetarian

**9** She enjoys dairy ______________ such as cheese, milk, etc.

   ⓐ consumers        ⓑ products        ⓒ gyms

**10** ______________ can't eat chicken, eggs or cheese. They only eat vegetables.

   ⓐ Joggers        ⓑ Fruitarians        ⓒ Vegans

## Listen to the dialogs and fill in the blanks.

**A**   **25** / Unit4
Listen and answer

W   Isn't it ___________ being vegan?  I'm a ___________ and it's hard for me to

find food I ___________ ___________ .  But at least I can eat ___________

and ___________ .

M   Sometimes it's ___________ but it's ___________ ___________ for my friend.

He's a fruitarian.

W   Really?  So all he eats is fruit all the time?

M   ___________ ___________ .  He eats ___________ fruit.  He can eat other

things though too.


**B**   **26** / Unit4
Listen and answer

W   Hey Jim.  How was your ___________ ___________ the doctor's office?

M   I'm ___________ ___________ but he said I need more vitamins

___________ ___________ ___________ .

W   That's an easy problem ___________ ___________ .  Just eat more

___________ , vegetables, and milk.

M   ___________ ___________ those three things.  I don't know what to do.

The food I like doesn't have all the ___________ I need.

## Listen to the passages and fill in the blanks.

**A** **27** / Unit4
Listen and answer

Do you know what the food pyramid is?  The food pyramid is a ___________ to

eating ___________.  It shows us the foods that make up ___________

___________ ___________.  Bread, cereals, rice, and pasta should be the biggest

part of ___________ ___________.  We need about 6-11 servings ___________

___________.  The second biggest part of our diet should be ___________.  We

need about 3-5 servings a day.  Next is ___________ since we need about 2-4

servings a day.  ___________ and ___________ are important too, but we

___________ need about 2-3 servings a day.  ___________ and ___________

like candy and chocolate should ___________ ___________ only once in a while.

**B** **28** / Unit4
Listen and answer

Vegetarians and vegans are some of the ___________ ___________ in the world.

___________ ___________ eat lots of fruits and vegetables.  They both also never

eat ___________ ___________.  Vegetarians and vegans have ___________

___________, but they have one ___________ ___________.  They both do not

eat animals, but vegetarians can eat food that ___________ ___________ an

animal.  Vegetarians can eat ___________, milk and honey.  Vegans won't

___________ ___________ nor will they eat anything that comes from

___________ ___________.

# Being Sick

SL3-05
MP3

## A Fill in the blanks with the right words in the box.

1. __________ injury, damage to your body

2. __________ cure, make good, make well

3. __________ feeling hurt because you're injured

4. __________ a doctor who performs surgery

5. __________ a stick that goes under your arm to help you walk

6. __________ when the bone is not whole

7. __________ to lose blood because of injury on your body

8. __________ enlarged, puffed up, bigger than normal

9. __________ the place in a hospital where people go if they need help right away

10. __________ an injury from getting hit, usually there's a purple mark

11. __________ to injure your ankle, wrist, or knee by twisting or straining

12. __________ a scratch, an injury where the top layer of skin was rubbed harshly

| ❶ bruise | ❷ scrape | ❸ surgeon | ❹ sprain |
|---|---|---|---|
| ❺ swollen | ❻ broken | ❼ bleed | ❽ crutch |
| ❾ painful | ❿ wound | ⓫ heal | ⓬ emergency room |

## B Choose the right words for the blanks.

**1** The surgeon closed the _____________ with three stitches.

   ⓐ wound            ⓑ pain            ⓒ sprain

**2** People say time _____________ all wounds.

   ⓐ injuries            ⓑ heals            ⓒ closes

**3** Breaking any bone in your body is very _____________.

   ⓐ swollen            ⓑ stressed            ⓒ painful

**4** She wore a cast on her _____________ arm.

   ⓐ bruised            ⓑ broken            ⓒ scratched

**5** I _____________ my ankle yesterday during the soccer game.

   ⓐ sprained            ⓑ cured            ⓒ healed

**6** Her eyes are _____________ because she cried a lot last night.

   ⓐ scratched            ⓑ swollen            ⓒ sprained

**7** The _____________ finished the operation in three hours.

   ⓐ technician            ⓑ nurse            ⓒ surgeon

**8** She fell down the stairs and got a _____________ on her leg.

   ⓐ mark            ⓑ crutch            ⓒ bruise

**9** I have been on _____________ for 3 months after tumbling down the stairs.

   ⓐ traps            ⓑ crutches            ⓒ heals

**10** I got this _____________ on my knee from falling off my bike.

   ⓐ bone            ⓑ scrape            ⓒ accident

## Listen to the dialogs and fill in the blanks.

**A**  **32** / Unit5
Listen and answer

W  Paul, you look uncomfortable.  ______________ ______________?

M  I ______________ ______________ the hospital yesterday.  The doctor said my

______________ ______________ because of the way ______________ ______________.

W  Your job may be ______________ ______________ your back.  You always

______________ long hours hunched ______________ ______________ ______________.

What did the doctor say?

M  I should ______________ ______________ ______________ my back ______________ and

not hunched over.


**B**  **33** / Unit5
Listen and answer

M  I'm ______________ ______________ anymore, Mom.  I ______________ ______________

to go to the hospital.

W  No, you've been ______________ for a week.  You should go to the hospital and

______________ ______________ ______________.  Then, you'll be OK.

M  I'm ______________ ______________ and I feel good today.

W  No way.  Look at you.  You're ______________ and you ______________

______________ ______________.  I'll take you to the hospital in 10 minutes.

If you get an ______________, your fever will ______________ ______________.

## Listen to the passages and fill in the blanks.

**A**  **34** / Unit5
Listen and answer

Have you ever been to the hospital before?  ____________ are very busy places.

The ____________ people at the hospital are the doctors in the emergency room.

The emergency room is ____________ you go if you need to be ____________

right away.  You don't go to the emergency room if you ____________

____________ ____________ .  People only go there if they have a ____________

____________ that can't wait.  Many of the ____________ in the emergency room

have been in a ____________ ____________ .


**B**  **35** / Unit5
Listen and answer

Usually when you call an ____________ , it only takes them a few minutes

____________ ____________ .  That's because ambulances drive very fast to

____________ ____________ people who need help.  Ambulances are also

____________ to go through ____________ ____________ .  All other drivers must

____________ ____________ ____________ the way for them.  The people who

drive the ambulance ____________ ____________ EMTs, Emergency Medical

Technician.  If you want to be an EMT, you must ____________ ____________

____________ just drive fast.  An EMT knows how to help someone that

____________ ____________ , having trouble ____________ or has ____________

from a ____________ .

# Unit 6 — Having Fun



**Vocabulary**

### A  Fill in the blanks with the right words in the box.

1  __________  to cry, yell

2  __________  pleasant, amusing

3  __________  the ability to do something well

4  __________  to encourage someone to do something

5  __________  your job or duty to do something

6  __________  to become a member of a group, club, etc.

7  __________  a person who is part of a group

8  __________  something you do that requires moving and being lively

9  __________  afraid, feeling frightened about something

10  __________  to do something over and over again to get good at it

11  __________  joint action by a group of people, everyone working together

12  __________  an activity you like to do in your free time

| | | | |
|---|---|---|---|
| ❶ cheer | ❷ scared | ❸ practice | ❹ fun |
| ❺ activity | ❻ join | ❼ member | ❽ scream |
| ❾ hobby | ❿ skill | ⓫ teamwork | ⓬ responsibility |

**B** **Choose the right words for the blanks.**

**1** What is your favorite outdoor ______________ ?

   ⓐ activity　　　　ⓑ movement　　　　ⓒ going

**2** It's my ______________ to take out the garbage every Sunday.

   ⓐ chance　　　　ⓑ mistake　　　　ⓒ responsibility

**3** Team sports require ______________ more than individual ability.

   ⓐ players　　　　ⓑ teammate　　　　ⓒ teamwork

**4** Let's go bungee jumping. It will be ______________ and exciting.

   ⓐ fun　　　　ⓑ scary　　　　ⓒ shocking

**5** I'm ______________ because I've never been on a roller coaster before.

   ⓐ puzzled　　　　ⓑ scared　　　　ⓒ funny

**6** He ______________ the violin for two hours every day.

   ⓐ practices　　　　ⓑ exercises　　　　ⓒ improves

**7** All the students are ______________ for their school's team.

   ⓐ yelling　　　　ⓑ shouting　　　　ⓒ cheering

**8** As the woman ______________ for help, the thief ran away.

   ⓐ scared　　　　ⓑ screamed　　　　ⓒ required

**9** Would you like to ______________ our book club? I'm sure you'll like it.

   ⓐ pay　　　　ⓑ sign　　　　ⓒ join

**10** He has a great ______________ in writing. I'm sure he'll be a great writer someday.

   ⓐ skill　　　　ⓑ attention　　　　ⓒ response

## Listen to the dialogs and fill in the blanks.

**A**  **39** / Unit6
Listen and answer

**W**  You read _____________ _____________ every day.  Are they that much

_____________ ?

**M**  I _____________ _____________ .  That's why _____________ _____________ comic

books are now movies.

**W**  You're right.  *X-men, Iron Man, The Hulk,* are all comic books.

**M**  _____________ _____________ are good, but the comic books _____________

_____________ .  I think it's _____________ _____________ _____________ books too.

**W**  I agree.  The book is always _____________ _____________ the movie.


**B**  **40**/ Unit6
Listen and answer

**M**  Do you want to go to the arcade _____________ _____________ ?  There's a

_____________ _____________ there.

**W**  No, I don't like video games.  What's the new game?

**M**  You can win _____________ _____________ .  Some are very cute and the game

_____________ _____________ .

**W**  I love stuffed animals!  I'll _____________ _____________ you.

**M**  Okay, but it's not easy _____________ _____________ .  We need a lot of money.

## Listen to the passages and fill in the blanks.

**A** **41** / Unit6
Listen and answer

Have you ever heard of the Boy Scouts?  It's a club that many young boys

___________ .  Right now there are about ___________ ___________ members.

Many people think Boy Scouts only learn ___________ ___________ .  It's true

that Boy Scouts do many outdoor activities like ___________ and ___________ .

But they also learn ___________ ___________ like ___________ ___________

and responsibility at the same time.  When Boy Scouts work together to make a fire

or ___________ ___________ a tent, they are learning more than just ___________

skills.  They're learning ___________ ___________ like ___________ .

**B** **42** / Unit6
Listen and answer

Does ___________ ___________ a bridge ___________ ___________ fun to you?

For some people, jumping off bridges and buildings is a fun ___________ .  It's

called bungee jumping.  Bungee jumping first started around the ___________

___________ .  Ever since then people have been ___________ ___________ new

and more exciting places to ___________ ___________ .  Bungee jumpers have

even jumped off the Eiffel Tower ___________ ___________ .  But before you start

jumping off the ___________ ___________ in your town, learn about bungee

jumping ___________ .  The most ___________ ___________ beginners make is

using a bungee rope that is ___________ ___________ .

# Festivals

SL3-07
**MP3**

**Vocabulary**

## A Fill in the blanks with the right words in the box.

1  __________  a meeting where people discuss a problem or topic

2  __________  a person who sells products on the street

3  __________  television, radio, or newspapers

4  __________  the process of getting something ready

5  __________  to do something enjoyable for a special occasion

6  __________  be present at a meeting or event

7  __________  the people who work for an organization

8  __________  someone who does a task without being asked

9  __________  relating to a country which is not yours

10  __________  clothing you wear for a special occasion

11  __________  an event in which people dress up and wear masks

12  __________  a procession of people or vehicles moving through a public place to celebrate an important day or event

| ❶ street vendor | ❷ media | ❸ seminar | ❹ preparation |
|---|---|---|---|
| ❺ masquerade | ❻ parade | ❼ staff | ❽ attend |
| ❾ volunteer | ❿ celebrate | ⓫ foreign | ⓬ costume |

# B Choose the right words for the blanks.

**1** During the _____________ tomorrow, we can debate on the matter.

ⓐ seminar  ⓑ movie  ⓒ parade

**2** I've been busy with _____________ for the trip.

ⓐ exercises  ⓑ definitions  ⓒ preparations

**3** What are you going to wear to the _____________ party?

ⓐ invite  ⓑ masquerade  ⓒ marching

**4** The road is blocked because people are marching in a _____________ .

ⓐ parade  ⓑ band  ⓒ building

**5** This is a notice for the entire _____________ from the president.

ⓐ hallway  ⓑ corner  ⓒ staff

**6** He couldn't _____________ the meeting because he wasn't invited.

ⓐ return  ⓑ attend  ⓒ arrive

**7** We need more _____________ to hand out food to the poor.

ⓐ volunteers  ⓑ homeless  ⓒ orphans

**8** All of my family gathered to _____________ Jacob's wedding.

ⓐ surprise  ⓑ present  ⓒ celebrate

**9** How many _____________ languages do you speak?

ⓐ special  ⓑ foreign  ⓒ favorite

**10** My _____________ was the scariest at the Halloween party.

ⓐ concert  ⓑ costume  ⓒ reporter

## Listen to the dialogs and fill in the blanks.

**A** **46** / Unit7
Listen and answer

M   Hi, I'm a ___________ with the Daily News.

I'm here for the press conference for the ___________ ___________.

W   You're a little ___________. Only security members are allowed

___________ ___________ ___________ right now.

Can I see your ___________ ___________ please?

M   Sure, here you go.

W   You ___________ ___________ in this room from 4-6. But it's only 3:30.

You're going to have to ___________ ___________.

**B** **47** / Unit7
Listen and answer

M   I'm going to ___________ next week with my father.

W   Really? Are you going to see the ___________ ___________?

M   No, my father's going to attend the ___________ ___________.

Actually he ___________ the festival every year, and ___________ I really

like books I told him to ___________ ___________ with him.

W   ___________ ___________ ___________ have a great time.

I ___________ I was going too.

## Listen to the passages and fill in the blanks.

**A** 48 / Unit7
Listen and answer

Festivals can ___________ tourists from all over the world.  The Cannes Film

Festival is ___________ ___________ , but people from all over the world come

to ___________ ___________ .  Some of these people are ___________

___________ too.  They come because The Cannes Film Festival is ___________

___________ ___________ film festival in the world.  Young filmmakers

___________ ___________ ___________ to show their movies to famous

___________ and producers.  The festival is a great ___________ for rising

___________ as well.  Many of today's big movie stars didn't ___________

___________ until they ___________ in a movie at the Cannes Film Festival.


**B** 49 / Unit7
Listen and answer

John is very ___________ for the ___________ festival tomorrow.  His town is

having a ___________ parade to ___________ .  There will be a ___________

___________ , balloons, and people dancing to music.  John is going to be part

of ___________ ___________ too.  He will be on one of the floats.  At first, he

was very ___________ about having a lot of people ___________ ___________

him.  Then John ___________ that it's a theater festival.  Everyone will be

___________ ___________ ___________ .  John will be wearing a costume too.

He also has a mask to ___________ ___________ ___________ .

# Unit 8 — Home Appliances



**Vocabulary**

**A** **Fill in the blanks with the right words in the box.**

1  __________  to clean with a mop

2  __________  a device that can heat a place

3  __________  mend; repair; to make good again

4  __________  a plate; what we use to put food on

5  __________  to make warm or hot

6  __________  an appliance that keeps food and drinks cold

7  __________  fixed tightly in a position and cannot move

8  __________  something you use to control a machine from far away

9  __________  to be out of order; to smash into smaller pieces, to split into parts

10  __________  a device that provides fire for cooking

11  __________  an appliance used to make food into a liquid

12  __________  a machine that washes and dries pans, cutlery, plates using electricity

| | | | |
|---|---|---|---|
| ❶ dishwasher | ❷ blender | ❸ radiator | ❹ gas stove |
| ❺ break | ❻ stuck | ❼ refrigerator | ❽ remote control |
| ❾ heat up | ❿ dish | ⓫ fix | ⓬ mop |

**1**  I accidentally dropped my cell phone and it ______________ .

ⓐ broke ⓑ wasted ⓒ throw

**2**  Please get me a cool drink from the ______________ .

ⓐ stove ⓑ cabinet ⓒ refrigerator

**3**  I was ______________ on the road because of a traffic jam.

ⓐ traveled ⓑ stuck ⓒ fixed

**4**  He used the ______________ to turn on the TV.

ⓐ channel ⓑ cable ⓒ remote control

**5**  You can ______________ the water on the gas stove.

ⓐ heat up ⓑ freeze ⓒ cool

**6**  The microwave is broken, so we need to ______________ it.

ⓐ buy ⓑ fix ⓒ renew

**7**  This winter is too cold. We need more ______________ in our office.

ⓐ radiators ⓑ microwaves ⓒ air conditioners

**8**  I had to ______________ the floor after I spilled my juice.

ⓐ sweep ⓑ mop ⓒ spread

**9**  I have a ______________ but I prefer to wash dishes by hand.

ⓐ freezer ⓑ blender ⓒ dishwasher

**10**  Let's use the ______________ to turn these bananas into a smoothie.

ⓐ blind ⓑ blender ⓒ washer

## Listen to the dialogs and fill in the blanks.

**A**  **53** / Unit8
Listen and answer

W  Hey Jim, there are sparks in your ____________.

M  What do you ____________ there are ____________?

W  I can see ____________ ____________ in your microwave.  It ____________ ____________ electricity.

M  Oh no!  That's because I put the food in a ____________ ____________.  Quick, ____________ the STOP button!

W  You need to be ____________ ____________.  You ____________ ____________ your microwave!

**B**  **54** / Unit8
Listen and answer

W  Hey Jim, I think your refrigerator ____________ ____________.  The milk ____________ ____________ anymore.

M  Oh really?  Well, it is an old refrigerator.

W  Are you ____________ you didn't ____________ ____________?  You know you're ____________ ____________ breaking things.

M  This time it ____________ ____________.  The refrigerator is just too old.  I've ____________ ____________ for a long time.

## Listen to the passages and fill in the blanks.

**55** / Unit8
Listen and answer

Everyone in Lisa's family likes to ______________ ______________ . Lisa likes tea

because ______________ ______________ her feel better.  However, for almost

______________ ______________ Lisa had to drink cold tea.  That's because

______________ ______________ was broken.  But Lisa's father finally ______________

the stove.  Now Lisa's family can make ______________ ______________ all day long.

But her family must be careful though.  If they ______________ the stove too much,

it will break again.  ______________ ______________ ______________ they broke the

stove before.  They used it all day long to ______________ ______________ the water.

**56** / Unit8
Listen and answer

Using a ______________ ______________ is very tiring.  They are usually big and

______________ . But now there is a new kind of vacuum cleaner.  It's called the

Roomba.  The Roomba is a robotic vacuum cleaner.  It moves all ______________

______________ and cleans your ______________ .  The Roomba is small and quiet

too.  The Roomba can even ______________ ______________ tables and chairs

blocking its way.  It never ______________ ______________ .  Also, the Roomba won't

______________ ______________ the stairs either.  It knows ______________ the stairs

are, so you don't have to ______________ ______________ it.  Just turn the Roomba

on and a few hours later, all of your floors will ______________ ______________ .

# Unit 9 — Environment

SL3-09
MP3



**A** **Fill in the blanks with the right words in the box.**

1 __________ trash; rubbish; waste

2 __________ to throw away; to get rid of

3 __________ to keep something or someone safe

4 __________ to damage or ruin something

5 __________ to move something apart

6 __________ substances made by a chemical process

7 __________ to change from a solid into a liquid

8 __________ a container in which people put trash

9 __________ the food that is left after a meal

10 __________ when something dirty is put in our environment

11 __________ the blackish gas given off when something burns

12 __________ to process something so that it can be used again

| | | | |
|---|---|---|---|
| ❶ destroy | ❷ litter | ❸ recycle | ❹ garbage |
| ❺ trash bin | ❻ chemical | ❼ melt | ❽ smoke |
| ❾ protect | ❿ pollution | ⓫ separate | ⓬ leftovers |

**B  Choose the right words for the blanks.**

**1**  Entering a university will ______________ me from my family.

   ⓐ gather       ⓑ refuse       ⓒ separate

**2**  Wear a helmet when you ride your bike to ______________ your head.

   ⓐ prohibit       ⓑ protect       ⓒ provide

**3**  The ice cube ______________ in the hot sun.

   ⓐ froze       ⓑ cooled       ⓒ melted

**4**  We need more ______________ to make the street clean.

   ⓐ trash       ⓑ chemicals       ⓒ trash bins

**5**  You should throw your ______________ in the trash can.

   ⓐ garbage       ⓑ stuff       ⓒ belongings

**6**  Be careful. If the police see you ______________ , you will be fined.

   ⓐ collecting       ⓑ littering       ⓒ wasting

**7**  If we ______________ waste paper, we can save a lot of money.

   ⓐ recycle       ⓑ regain       ⓒ restart

**8**  The earthquake ______________ all the houses and roads in town.

   ⓐ saved       ⓑ broke       ⓒ destroyed

**9**  ______________ rose from the roof of the burning house.

   ⓐ Hail       ⓑ Smoke       ⓒ Wind

**10**  Sometimes it is hard to breath because of all the air ______________ .

   ⓐ condition       ⓑ movement       ⓒ pollution

## Listen to the dialogs and fill in the blanks.

**A** **60** / Unit9
Listen and answer

W   Wow, last weekend was _____________ _____________ . The newspaper said

it was _____________ _____________ Celsius.

M   Did you see the documentary on polar bears last night? _____________

_____________ because so much Arctic ice _____________ _____________ .

W   I watched it, too. It was _____________ _____________ seeing all of those

_____________ polar bears.

M   We should try to _____________ _____________ _____________ , or we might be

in _____________ _____________ like those polar bears.

**B** **61** / Unit9
Listen and answer

M   I'm going to start walking _____________ _____________ now. I want to

_____________ our natural resources.

W   That's a good idea. We should all use _____________ _____________ . I'm

going to stop _____________ _____________ .

M   That's great. Trees are an important _____________ _____________ too. Let's

also _____________ our plastics.

W   Okay, but plastic is not a natural resource. We make plastic using many

different _____________ . Natural resources are things found _____________

_____________ .

## Listen to the passages and fill in the blanks.

**A**  **62** / Unit9
Listen and answer

Most trash can be ___________ ___________ or ___________ . For example,

metal cans can be recycled.  New cans can be ___________ ___________ the old

ones.  That is why it is important to ___________ your cans in the right place.

There are special ___________ ___________ for cans.  Glass is another thing that

can be recycled.  Old glass ___________ ___________ until it ___________ .

Recycling glass is ___________ ___________ than making new glass from sand.

Even food can be used again.  The leftover food can be used to make compost.

Compost will ___________ the soil ___________ and help the plants grow.


**B**  **63** / Unit9
Listen and answer

Global warming ___________ ___________ a big problem.  Pollution from

factories and cars is making the world ___________ .  Many factories

___________ a lot of smoke and chemicals.  These things make our ___________

___________ .  The gases from cars are bad for the environment too.  They

___________ the ozone.  The ozone ___________ the Earth from the sun.

Without the ozone, the sun will feel too hot.  If the Earth gets too hot, we won't be

able to go outside.  Plants and animals ___________ ___________ if the Earth is

too hot.  All of your favorite flowers will start ___________ ___________ .

**Vocabulary**

SL3-10
MP3

**A** **Fill in the blanks with the right words in the box.**

1 ________ a thousand million

2 ________ to decide or choose by using a ballot

3 ________ to successfully complete a course

4 ________ a person who designs clothes as a job

5 ________ a person who works in business

6 ________ wealthy; having a lot of money

7 ________ an organization that collects money to help people

8 ________ author; a person who writes stories, novels

9 ________ a person who knows the law and represents people in court

10 ________ a member of a female religious community

11 ________ someone who has the highest position in a group or country

12 ________ to be in charge of something; to organize something such as a business

| | | | |
|---|---|---|---|
| ❶ lawyer | ❷ charity | ❸ rich | ❹ graduate |
| ❺ writer | ❻ run | ❼ billion | ❽ businessman |
| ❾ vote | ❿ nun | ⓫ president | ⓬ fashion designer |

## Choose the right words for the blanks.

1. The _____________ has a lot of best-selling books.

   ⓐ fool　　　　　　ⓑ journal　　　　　　ⓒ writer

2. Christian Dior is one of the world famous _____________.

   ⓐ amateurs　　　　ⓑ inventors　　　　　ⓒ fashion designers

3. Mother Teresa is a _____________, and she taught children at church.

   ⓐ nun　　　　　　ⓑ preacher　　　　　ⓒ priest

4. When I was young, I wanted to be the _____________ of the USA.

   ⓐ owner　　　　　ⓑ president　　　　　ⓒ staff

5. My dream is to _____________ a toy store.

   ⓐ save　　　　　　ⓑ produce　　　　　ⓒ run

6. Which university did you _____________ from?

   ⓐ graduate　　　　ⓑ enter　　　　　　ⓒ separate

7. Someday I will set up a _____________ to help the poor and the old.

   ⓐ school　　　　　ⓑ orphanage　　　　ⓒ charity

8. A millionaire is a very _____________ person.

   ⓐ famous　　　　　ⓑ rich　　　　　　ⓒ poor

9. We hired a _____________ after we got into a car accident.

   ⓐ lawyer　　　　　ⓑ judge　　　　　　ⓒ jury

10. The _____________ left the company to start a new job at a bank.

    ⓐ farmer　　　　　ⓑ child　　　　　　ⓒ businessman

## Listen to the dialogs and fill in the blanks.

**A** 67 / Unit10
Listen and answer

M   Hi Lisa.  Do you know how the Nobel Prize ___________ ?

W   Of course.  Alfred Nobel, the famous inventor, wanted to ___________

     ___________ ___________ to people who did something great.  Every year

     Nobel Prizes ___________ ___________ ___________ congratulate them.

M   How was Alfred Nobel so rich?  I thought that many scientists ___________

     ___________ .

W   Well, he was ___________ ___________ .  He invented dynamite and also

     ___________ a factory.

**B** 68 / Unit10
Listen and answer

M   Did you know that Walt Disney was the ___________ voice of Mickey Mouse?

W   Really?  No, I didn't know that.  I thought he was just a ___________

     ___________ .  When he smiles, he does ___________ ___________ Mickey

     Mouse though.

M   His ___________ ___________ said that Walt Disney also gave Mickey Mouse

     his ___________ .

W   Walt Disney must have been a ___________ and ___________ person.

## Listen to the passages and fill in the blanks.

**69** / Unit10
Listen and answer

There are many ways to help poor people.  We can ____________ money, food,

and clothes from others and then ____________ ____________ to the poor.  But

some people help the poor ____________ ____________ their own money.  Bill

Gates is one of those people.  He used ____________ of dollars of his own

money to start a ____________ .  His charity is called the Bill and Melinda Gates

foundation.  Melinda is Bill Gates' wife.  ____________ ____________ the charity

together.  At least one billion dollars ____________ ____________ ____________

every year to ____________ ____________ all over the world.  Millions of dollars

have been given away to countries ____________ ____________ .


**70** / Unit10
Listen and answer

Aesop was a writer in ____________ ____________ .  He is famous for his fables,

which are stories that teach a ____________ ____________ .  All of his fables are

short, simple stories for children.  One of his most ____________ fables is *The

Ant and the Grasshopper*.  It's a story about a ____________ ant and a lazy

grasshopper.  The ant worked hard every day during the summer finding food.

The grasshopper just played all day long.  When winter came, the ant had

____________ ____________ food to eat.  The grasshopper didn't have any food to

eat. The ____________ of the story is to ____________ ____________ the future.

# Natural Disasters

**Vocabulary**

SL3-11
MP3

**A** **Fill in the blanks with the right words in the box.**

1 __________ whole; total; full

2 __________ a shaking of the ground

3 __________ ice that falls from the sky

4 __________ to burst forth, release, eject matter

5 __________ within; the inner part; opposite of outside

6 __________ a very serious accident; a very bad event

7 __________ a mountain from which lava can come out

8 __________ a place that is safe from the rain, snow, etc.

9 __________ someone who has been hurt or killed

10 __________ a large fire that grows quickly and is hard to put out

11 __________ when there is so much water that it flows onto dry land

12 __________ to quickly move something backwards and forwards or up and down

| | | | |
|---|---|---|---|
| ❶ victim | ❷ shake | ❸ volcano | ❹ disaster |
| ❺ erupt | ❻ entire | ❼ earthquake | ❽ inside |
| ❾ hail | ❿ wildfire | ⓫ shelter | ⓬ flood |

**1**  Our organization is raising money for the ______________ of the flood.

ⓐ victims                    ⓑ criminals                    ⓒ creators

**2**  If you ______________ a bottle of chocolate milk, it tastes better.

ⓐ separate                   ⓑ sparkle                      ⓒ shake

**3**  The storm was a ______________. Many houses were damaged.

ⓐ nature                     ⓑ injury                       ⓒ disaster

**4**  A ______________ can be dangerous if it erupts.

ⓐ hail                       ⓑ volcano                      ⓒ storm

**5**  Lava comes out of a volcano when it ______________.

ⓐ shakes                     ⓑ erupts                       ⓒ builds

**6**  He was so hungry that he ate the ______________ pizza.

ⓐ entire                     ⓑ small                        ⓒ full

**7**  What is ______________ your bag?

ⓐ into                       ⓑ inside                       ⓒ outside

**8**  The ______________ covered the whole field of crops with water.

ⓐ hail                       ⓑ flood                        ⓒ drought

**9**  The school was used as a ______________ for the earthquake victims.

ⓐ restaurant                 ⓑ shelter                      ⓒ mansion

**10**  The ______________ in the forest burned down half of the trees.

ⓐ wildfire                   ⓑ earthquake                   ⓒ drought

## Listen to the dialogs and fill in the blanks.

**A**  **74** / Unit11
Listen and answer

W    Have you ever been in a ______________ ______________ before?  It's very

______________ .

M    No, I haven't.  Why is it scary?  How is it different from a snow storm?

W    Hail is when ______________ ______________ from the sky.  If the storm is bad,

the ice can be ______________ ______________ ______________ baseballs.

M    Really?  That sounds dangerous.  Hail that big can probably ______________

______________ ______________ .


**B**  **75** / Unit11
Listen and answer

W    There was a ______________ in the forest yesterday.  Two campers were

______________ ______________ ______________ when it happened.

M    I ______________ about it on the news.  The wind made the fire ______________

to be very big.

W    Yeah, it helped the fire to grow ______________ ______________ .

Why are there so many wildfires in the summer and ______________ ?

M    The hot weather and ______________ ______________ makes it easy to

______________ ______________ ______________ .

## Listen to the passages and fill in the blanks.

**A** **76** / Unit11
Listen and answer

_______________ _______________ are a problem in America.  Many people

_______________ _______________ their homes to tornadoes and _______________.

That is why the United States _______________ FEMA.  FEMA was made to help the

_______________ _______________ natural disasters.  FEMA helps them _______________

_______________ food, shelter, and clothes.  But FEMA only helps people in the

U.S.  And natural disasters _______________ all over the world.  This is why the

_______________ _______________ is so important.  The Red Cross is _______________

_______________ FEMA.  They help people in different countries all over the world.

**B** **77** / Unit11
Listen and answer

Have you ever seen a _______________ before?  It looks like a mountain but it's very

different.  A volcano has a _______________ _______________ at the top.  This opening

is a _______________ _______________ where lava can _______________ _______________.

Lava comes from _______________ _______________ the earth.  It looks like orange

water.  But be careful.  Lava is very hot!  It's as hot _______________ _______________.

When a volcano erupts, lava comes out from the top.  Sometimes _______________

_______________ _______________ of lava will come out.  This lava can _______________ an

_______________ town.

# Unit 12 — Outer Space

**Vocabulary**

## A Fill in the blanks with the right words in the box.

1. _________ to move around something

2. _________ creatures from outer space

3. _________ to damage or destroy with fire

4. _________ the area outside the earth's atmosphere

5. _________ a round object in space moving around a star

6. _________ the sun and the planets going around it

7. _________ a person who is trained to travel in a spacecraft

8. _________ a long instrument that helps us to see distant things

9. _________ a bright object with a long tail that travels around the sun

10. _________ a scientist who studies the stars, planets, and other objects in space

11. _________ an object that is sent into space to collect information

12. _________ a piece of rock or metal that burns brightly when it enters the earth's atmosphere from space

| | | | |
|---|---|---|---|
| ❶ meteor | ❷ outer space | ❸ planet | ❹ astronaut |
| ❺ alien | ❻ satellite | ❼ telescope | ❽ solar system |
| ❾ burn | ❿ orbit | ⓫ comet | ⓬ astronomer |

**1** We went up to Canada to watch the ______________ showers.

   ⓐ meteor       ⓑ star       ⓒ moon

**2** Do you think there'll be life on another ______________ like Mars?

   ⓐ comet       ⓑ planet       ⓒ meteor

**3** Do you know who the first ______________ on the moon was?

   ⓐ alien       ⓑ astronomer       ⓒ astronaut

**4** They are telecasting the game now live via ______________.

   ⓐ satellite       ⓑ telescope       ⓒ microscope

**5** We can see the stars using a ______________.

   ⓐ telescope       ⓑ microscope       ⓒ phonograph

**6** There're nine planets in our ______________.

   ⓐ spaceship       ⓑ solar system       ⓒ outer space

**7** Most of the trees were ______________ down in a wildfire.

   ⓐ erupted       ⓑ flooded       ⓒ burnt

**8** ______________ are always trying to find new planets and stars.

   ⓐ Aliens       ⓑ Astronomers       ⓒ Astronauts

**9** A meteor enters the earth's atmosphere from ______________.

   ⓐ earth's surface       ⓑ solar system       ⓒ outer space

**10** In many sci-fi movies, the ______________ from outer space have green skin and big eyes.

   ⓐ spaceships       ⓑ aliens       ⓒ rockets

## Listen to the dialogs and fill in the blanks.

**A** **81** / Unit12
Listen and answer

W Thanks.  I learned a lot of __________ __________ about the planets and

the __________ __________ from your book.

M My pleasure.  So, which __________ is your favorite?  Mine's __________.

W I really like __________.  A lot of science fiction movies have __________

from Mars.  Why do you like Saturn?

M I like the __________ around it.  It looks like the planet __________

__________ a belt.


**B** **82** / Unit12
Listen and answer

W I wish there were more __________.  I really like the __________ trail of

light they __________ in the sky.

M There are many meteors __________ around __________ all the time.  We

just can't see them.

W Why?  Are they too small for us to see?

M Most of them __________ __________ before they are __________

__________ for us to see.

They burn up because they are very hot __________ __________ so fast.

**Listen to the passages and fill in the blanks.**

**83** / Unit12
Listen and answer

Everyone knows that the moon orbits around the Earth.  This means that the

moon ____________ ____________ the Earth ____________ ____________.  But did

you know that there are things orbiting the sun too?  Something that travels

around the sun is called a ____________.  A comet looks like a ____________

____________.  But a comet is actually ice, ____________ and ____________.

Comets look like they have a ____________ ____________.  The most famous

comet is Halley's Comet.  It's famous because you don't need a ____________ to

see it.  But you ____________ ____________ ____________ it once every 75 years.


**84** / Unit12
Listen and answer

____________ ____________ 20, 1969 Neil Armstrong became the ____________

____________ to walk on the moon.  But he didn't go there ____________.  There

were two other people with him.  Going to the moon ____________ ____________.

The ____________ had to ____________ for a long time.  Neil Armstrong was a

____________ for many years before he ____________ ____________ space.  He

almost ____________ ____________ ____________ become astronaut.  Neil

____________ ____________ his application a week late!  Neil Armstrong is

____________ ____________ today.  We can see him sometimes on TV.

# Memo

# Memo

# Memo

Level 3

# START Listening

The **Start Listening** series is a three-level listening program targeted towards young English learners. It is aimed to help students overcome the problems with understanding a native English speaker. By integrating real-life situations with a systematic learning approach, this series will boost the skills and confidence of everyone who is ready to start listening.

## FEATURES

- A creative approach that focuses on comprehension as much as listening
- Real-life situations to increase one's understanding of common and practical English
- An emphasis on the aspects of English that contribute most to intelligibility, particularly being able to understand long stretches of speech
- A wide range of entertaining topics from movies and music to science and technology
- Unique and engaging content that will facilitate self-study
- Audio Recordings by native English speakers
- A workbook which includes vocabulary tests and dictations
- Step by Step Process

## COMPONENTS

- Student Book
- Workbook
- MP3 files
- Answer Keys

Download Resources at **www.wcbooks.co.kr**

**WorldCom Edu**
www.wcbooks.co.kr